Dedication

This book is dedicated to my wife, Mary, and our children. I love you.

In addition, this book is dedicated to the next generations of citizens in the United States of America. There will always be a need to watch and improve our government. I hope that you will continue to keep our sovereign nation independent and strong. I also hope you will keep the fire of liberty burning in the U.S.A. There are checks and balances in our government. These checks and balances only work if citizens are involved in our government. I encourage you to participate in our government because you are the government.

This book is also dedicated to the U.S. Military and our veterans. Without you, I would not have the freedom to write this book.

Acknowledgments & Thanks

While there are many people that I owe a debt of gratitude for encouraging me in my life and for help, the following individuals, in particular deserve my deep <u>thanks</u>:

To my late mother, Gertrude Kafkas, who encouraged me, and loved me as only a mother loves a son;

To my late father, Dan Kafkas, for telling me he loved me and that he was proud of me;

To my late uncle, Dr. Thomas Poulos, for being one of my role models and for his encouragement with my education;

To my sister, Betty Saites, for her loving encouragement with my education and my other goals;

To my "uncle," Mario Kafkas, for his kindness, help and guidance;

To my friend and mentor, Peter Latsoudis, for our many discussions on politics, finance, banking, life and religion; for his example of service to the Church and humility; and for his encouragement and inspiration;

To my cousin, Bill Johnson, for his example of analyzing our government, and for our discussions on politics, law, Federal Reserve, banking, life and religion;

To my cousin, John Gianopolos, for his example of a keen business sense and friendship to others, and for our discussions on life, business, politics and family;

To the Franklin Public Library's Writers' Group for its encouragement with my writing; and

To the Franklin Public Library in Franklin, WI for its excellent public services.

Important Disclaimer Notice:

This book is <u>only</u> for very general historical, government analysis, and educational information.

This book is **not** legal, financial or accounting advice. This book should absolutely not be used in any way regarding any legal, financial or accounting or other decision. Readers are strongly advised to get the advice of a skilled attorney, skilled financial advisor, skilled accountant, and other professional.

The book's analysis is just one subjective analysis. There are other analyzes. The readers are strongly encouraged to research all topics themselves and to make up their own minds.

Typos and factual errors can occur. Things also change very rapidly and information can be outdated. The author and publisher cannot guarantee the accuracy of the information. In addition, absolutely no information or analysis in this book should be relied upon for any matter of any kind.

The author and the publisher make no representation or warranties of any kind, express or implied, about the completeness, accuracy, reliability, or suitability of this book or any information in this book for any particular purpose.

No warranty of any kind may be created in any way by any sales representative or sales materials.

About the Author

Theodore D. Kafkas, J.D., is an attorney in Wisconsin with more than 20 years of legal experience. His experience includes Constitutional law, financial law, real estate law, estate planning and general practice. He also worked in finance, Wisconsin government and other positions.

In addition, Atty. Kafkas wrote numerous published articles, provided many public presentations, and spoke before the Wisconsin Supreme Court and many other courts.

Atty. Kafkas earned his Juris Doctorate Degree from Marquette University Law School. While in law school, he was a Research Assistant to an Associate Dean/Law Professor.

Atty. Kafkas earned his Bachelor of Business Administration Degree, Summa cum Laude, from the University of Wisconsin-Milwaukee. Within his Bachelor of Business Administration Degree, Theodore Kafkas completed a Real Estate & Urban Development Major and a Finance Major.

Table of Contents

CHAPTER 1

ONE OF THE MAIN CAUSES OF THE ECONOMIC CRISIS - TECHNOLOGY

What are the main causes of the current economic crisis?

Technology can be a great asset to business and people. We are still in the beginning of an Information Age of technology.

The transition into an Information Age is not only affecting our businesses and people, but is also affecting our greater macro-economy.

Not realizing that large changes in technology will affect the macro-economy causes a lot of problems to societies. If the United States does not realize the effect, it cannot plan for, or correctly deal with, the effect.

Other factors such as the incorrect economic policies, huge U.S. debt, terrible Federal Reserve, unlimited financial influence in government elections, deregulation of the financial and banking industries, alleged stock/financial market manipulations, and international banking also affect our macro-economy. These will also be considered later in this book.

First, let's discuss one of the main topics of this book: Technology changes affects U.S. and world macro-economics.

When society has transition changes in technological ages, such as from the Agricultural Age to the Industrial Age (which I describe as post-internal combustion engines and post-electrical motors), and from the Industrial Age to the Information Age (which I describe as post computer), there are corresponding transitional changes in the macro-economy.

Think of these technology ages as steps.

The following graph demonstrates the steps of some technology ages.

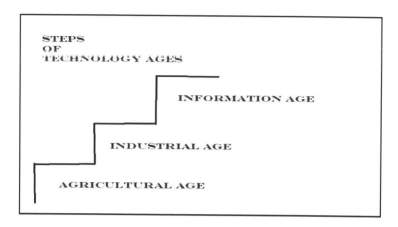

In the past, the U.S. has seen changes in technology steps and corresponding changes in the economy

For example, when a farmer in the early part of the 20th Century began to compete with an internal combustion engine-driven tractor to plow land, the farmer with the horse-drawn plow was at a disadvantage. Easily, one farmer with an internal combustion engine tractor could produce as much food as many farmers with horse drawn plows could produce. In addition, we know that the farmer with the tractor could produce more food at a lower cost. Also, the farmer with the tractor would be generally willing to sell his agriculture for a price less than the farmer with the horse. Many farmers eventually got internal combustion engine tractors or went out of business.

The same scenario would be true for an industrial manufacturer of cloths in competition with a foot-pedaled sewing machine/hand-tailor. Hand tailors could not produce as much clothing as industrial clothing manufacturers. In addition, hand tailors could not produce clothing at the same cost as industrial clothing manufactures. Therefore, almost all hand-tailors went out of business.

These are just a few examples. Of course, many other businesses went through a transformation during the Industrial revolution.

Technology gained during the transition from the Agricultural Age to the Industrial Age caused a decreased demand for workers at the same time that there was increased production in the world.

Many people were out of work during the Great Depression of the Industrial Age. At the same time, our country could produce much more than ever before.

During the Industrial Age, companies used assembly lines to leverage human labor.

In addition, during this Great Depression, some people were becoming very wealthy.

For example, Henry Ford became very wealthy with manufacturing automobiles.[1]

John D. Rockefeller also made a large amount of money with oil.[2] (Obviously, oil was needed for engines and other technology during the Industrial Age and is still needed today. Later in this book, I will further discuss the topic of oil.)

As our economy was adjusting to the Industrial Age, people wanted cars, but not everyone could afford a car.

For many people out of work, they could not even afford food.

There were "<u>soup lines</u>" at the same time that there were "<u>assembly lines</u>."

Therefore, the demand to buy food and many other items was lower than it could have been because of the high unemployment and because many people did not have money.

During the Industrial Age, there were also many home foreclosures and runs on banks.

Unmanaged, the macro-economy did not adjust. Instead, the macro-economy busted into the Great Depression. Those were very tough times for many millions of people.

Then, there were adjustments in public policies and laws. Safer working conditions, Worker's Compensation, Unemployment Compensation, wage and hour standards, unions, and special regulations with regards to child labor were eventually created and implemented.

What were these adjustments in public policy and laws doing to capitalism? A more absolute form of capitalism was modified in order to deal with the changes from the Agricultural Age to the Industrial Age.

Now, we are going through another technological change. We are going from the Industrial Age to the Information Age.

We are also going through another corresponding change in the macro-economy.

Does history repeat itself?

In the Information Age, computers, robotics, the Internet, science, engineering, biology, chemistry, etc., have resulted in an increased ability to produce more and at a lower cost. These changes are not happening in one day, but the changes are happening very quickly. We might not notice the effect that the Information Age is having on jobs unless we take some time to consider some of the changes in jobs.

For example, compared to 35 years ago, attorneys do not need as many people to type because of computers and word processing templates. Companies also do not need as many people to answer telephones because of computerized voice mail systems.

In addition, robotics, 3-D printing, and other computer technology have resulted in fewer employees needed to work in factories, banks and many other businesses. For example, a computer numerical control (CNC) machinist can do much more production than a regular non-CNC industrial machinist. We might not notice the growth of robotics in factories unless we travel into factories or research the growth of robotics.

All technology does not work as expected.

Here is a little funny side-story that got me thinking about changes in technology that are not expected.

I went into a restroom and the computerized sensors turned on the lights. I went into a bathroom stall. As I was about to leave the bathroom stall, the lights went off. Waiving my hands would not help because the bathroom stall's walls blocked the motion detector sensors. At the time, I was thinking how nice that manual light switch on the wall was in the past.

It makes me laugh now!

But, I am glad that these automatic lights are saving energy, saving financial resources for better uses, and reducing environmental pollution.

Eventually, robots and computers will do much more

work in the world.

We heard it when we were kids. Now, it is starting to become reality.

For instance, we can extrapolate that robots, driver-less vehicles, drones and computers will soon be doing almost every work in businesses and homes. Operational leverage of the labor force will continue to increase exponentially with technology.

Unless something big changes, the number of medical, pharmaceutical, chemistry, physics and other science innovations will continue to grow.

In addition, one technology also helps another technology to grow. Innovations build upon other inventions.

Since information technology in the Information Age makes the flow of innovations/inventions easier, the growth of technology will happen more quickly. For example, with the Internet, people can learn about new inventions quickly. People can also collaborate in different parts of the world and build on each others' ideas to make new innovations. Therefore, one invention or innovation could replace many jobs in a very short time.

There will continue to be a decreased need for workers (labor demand).

If we think about it, we are already seeing robotics in our everyday life with banks' automated teller machines (ATMs), DVD rental box machines, etc. So, there is less need for bank tellers and less need for video stores.

Likewise, email and faxes have resulted in less U.S. Postal mail/letters. Therefore, the need for postal workers has decreased and the U.S. Post Office has talked about closing some post offices.

Because of the Internet, online businesses need less salespeople. People also can watch newer movies online. In addition, instead of people buying paper books printed by people working for printing companies, people can buy electronic books online.

Technology changes have made commerce much more global. For example, satellite technology has resulted in people being able to instantly see and speak with other people across the world.

This communication technology resulted in an increase in global competition of labor and products. For instance, many of us had someone from across the world even provide technological support and even take over our computers to fix our problems via online connections.

The Information Age also has caused changes to people's health and lifespan. For example, the increases in medical technology have caused an increase in the world population which resulted in not only in an increased demand for products, but also in an important increased numbers of potential workers. People now can live longer and healthier with pace-makers, MRI diagnostics, CT scans, robotic surgery, new pharmacology, an abundance of food, etc. Since people live healthier and longer because of technology, people can work longer.

(As a side note, I find some things coincidental, interesting and humorous. It is commonly known that Steve "Jobs" and Bill "Gates" were Information Age leaders in computers. Does anyone see how technology has changed the "jobs" in this world? Did anyone else notice how much the "gates" to new technology have opened in this world?)

Furthermore, in 1800, the population of the world was approximately 1 billion.[3] In 2011, the population of the world was estimated to be 7 billion.[4] In 2045, the population of the world is projected to be 9 billion.[5]

The following two charts illustrate these populations and corresponding years.

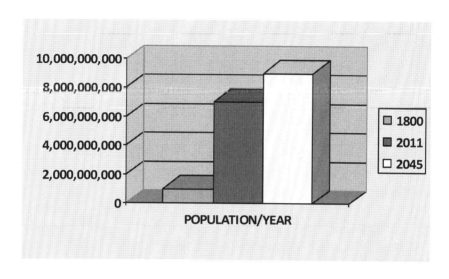

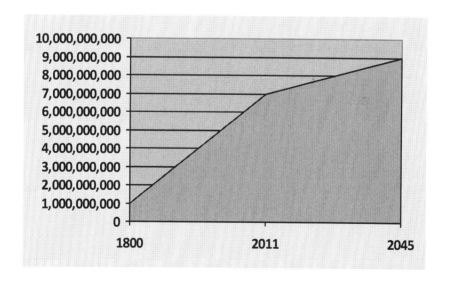

The U.S. population is also still growing. According to

the U.S. Census Web site, "The United States population on July 4, 2013 was: 316,225,499."[6] On May 15, 2014, I watched the Census Web site's U.S. population rise to 318,046,618.[7] Therefore, in less than one year during this time, the official U.S. population increased by almost 2 million people. Again, on Feb. 4th, 2017, I watched the U.S. population rise to 324,485,840.[8] Therefore, from July 4, 2013 to Feb. 4th, 2017, the official U.S. population increased by more than 8,000,000 people in about 3½ years.

So, as we examined, on one hand, we have technological advanced businesses that have the ability to produce more with less workers than before because of robotics and other efficiencies. *Therefore, there is a decreased demand for employees.*

On the other hand, and at the same time, the world population and U.S. population have both grown. Technological advances also gave people the ability to live and work longer. *Therefore, there is an increased supply of potential employees.*

This Information Age step has a double impact on employment *supply* and *demand* of workers.

These supply and demand changes are creating an employment bubble.

Imagine how many people in the U.S.A. and throughout the world are being affected by the technology changes. The impacts are staggering.

The employment bubble is already massive and growing.

As of May 5, 2014, there were approximately 1,274,710 unemployed workers in California who have run out of all available unemployment insurance benefits.[9] Incredibly, during this time, more than one million unemployed workers ran out unemployment insurance benefits in just one of our 50 states in the United States of America!

What about the official U.S. unemployment rate improving recently?

The United States Dept. of Labor, Bureau of Labor Statistics' website indicates,

> "**U-3**, total unemployed, as a percent of the civilian labor force (this is the definition used for the **official unemployment rate**);
> U-4, total unemployed plus discouraged workers, as a percent of the civilian labor force plus discouraged workers;
> U-5, total unemployed, plus discouraged workers, plus all other marginally attached workers, as a percent of the civilian labor force plus all marginally attached workers; and
> U-6, total unemployed, plus all marginally attached workers, plus total employed part time for economic reasons, as a percent of the civilian labor force plus all marginally attached workers.
>
> **Definitions** for the economic characteristics underlying the three broader measures of labor underutilization are worth mentioning here. Discouraged workers (U-4, U-5, and U-6 measures) are persons who are not in the labor force, want and are available for work, and had looked for a job sometime in the prior 12 months. They are <u>not counted</u> as unemployed because they had not searched for work in the prior 4 weeks, for the specific reason that they believed no jobs were available for them. The marginally attached (U-5 and U-6 measures) are a group that includes discouraged workers. The criteria for the marginally attached are the same as for discouraged workers, with the exception that any

reason could have been cited for the lack of job search in the prior 4 weeks. Persons employed part time for economic reasons (U-6 measure) are those working less than 35 hours per week who want to work full time, are available to do so, and gave an economic reason (their hours had been cut back or they were unable to find a full-time job) for working part time. These individuals are sometimes referred to as involuntary part-time workers."[10] (Emphasis added.)

The 2016 annual average (percent) of the U-6 unemployment rate for the United States was **9.6%**.[11]

Clearly, the U-6 is a more accurate estimate than some other estimates. But, the U-6 is not what we usually hear on the news.

Is the U-6 fully accurate? No.

But, do we trust the politicians to have their agents provide the true estimate? I don't. Do we trust the mainstream news media? I don't.

Louis Jacobson wrote in his article entitled, *PolitiFact: President's claim on unemployment rate is true, but has caveats*, found in the Tampa Bay Times January 23, 2015 online edition,

> "[T]he U-6 rate — unlike the more basic unemployment rate — hasn't returned to its pre-financial crisis level. The December U-6 rate was 11.2 percent, which is higher than the 11 percent rate in September 2008 . . ."[12]
> (Emphasis added.)

Part-time, low paying, jobs are not what people need to support their families. Many part-time jobs also do not have employee benefits like health insurance.

Jacobson also points out that,

"Additionally, while economists cheer the clear improvement in the basic unemployment rate, they also fret that a portion of that improvement stems from Americans leaving the labor market rather than finding jobs after experiencing joblessness. . . .

A way to measure this is by looking at a statistic called the labor force participation rate, which measures the number of people in the labor force divided by the civilian, noninstitutionalized population. The labor force shrinks when someone retires, voluntarily gives up working (such as when they become a full-time parent or go back to school full time) or *because they simply give up hope of finding a job*.

The labor force participation rate has decreased markedly since 2008. In September 2008, it stood at 66.0 percent, but fell to 62.7 percent in December. *It's now at its lowest point since the late 1970s*, a time when fewer women were working."[13]

It is a tragedy that some people that are fully capable of working are to the point that they are giving up hope of finding a job.

Just like in the Great Depression, there is an employment bubble now. In addition, just like in the Great Depression, the corresponding changes in the supply and demand of world labor are also negatively affecting the macro-economy now.

Ignoring the impact of the employment bubble on our macro-economy is too big of a risk for our country. We need to recognize the issues. Technology change is one of the <u>largest factors</u> negatively affecting our macro-economy because it is not being properly addressed.

Recognizing that human jobs have been, and will continue to be, lost to technology leads to the correct focus for our macro-economic analysis.

Think of part of the macro-economy as a wheel with workers in the center. Imagine the demand for products and services on top of the wheel. Picture the supply for products and services on the bottom of the circle. The continuous flow of the demand and supply around the circle helps to illustrate that ***<u>jobs</u> spread wealth* and *affect both supply and demand.***

Where do technology changes fit in the wheel? Just like any tool could also be imagined in the wheel, technology changes invisibly fit in the middle with the worker. The technological advances make the worker much more efficient at production and allow the worker to produce more.

The following diagram (wheel) illustrates that demand, supply and workers are strongly related to each other. Demand, supply and workers are also keeping the macro-economy rolling along. But, when this wheel's supply and demand are not economically balanced, the wheel turns into an imploding, downward, spiral.

Less Workers
=
Less
Consumers
(Demand)

Workers
=
Producers
(Supply)

Economy Not Balanced

Technology
that Produces
=
Less Workers

Workers
Produce
Technology
that helps
Produces
More

The high-tech companies can leverage technology and workers to make and sell products and/or services that are efficient, convenient, can do more, are sold at a lower cost, and/or have other improvements. Therefore, some high-tech companies and market niches may do very well for years.

However, even at a lower cost, if many people do not have family-supporting jobs, they will not have the money to buy (demand) products that are manufactured (supply). In addition, if many people do not have jobs, they will pull money from savings, investments, etc. At the same time, the macro-economy will eventually suffer when a large portion of the unemployed population will not be able to pay their mortgages, not be able to pay their car payments, and/or will go bankrupt.

Again, technological changes of the Information Age are causing a blow to the macro-economy. This should be one of nation's major focal points, but no one is adequately dealing with this topic.

If the technology changes' effects on the macro-economy are not addressed, the macro-economy has an eventual risk of collapsing. At the least, eventually, the entire rolling macro-economic will slow because the unemployed will not be able to participate in purchasing (demanding) goods. More, there will be a loss of individual economic independence as more people cannot support themselves.

The Federal Reserve, government officials, politicians, economists and the news commentators are not seeing, or at least by far not discussing, the issue that technology changes are drastically affecting the macro-economy and causing a huge employment bubble.

More, we need to immediately analyze this real issue, recognize the true implications and effects now, and make strategies and plans to effectively deal with the changes and employment bubble with our core values and logic.

The root issue of the technology changes from the Information Age negatively affecting the unemployment rate which led to trouble in our macro-economy was _not_ correctly addressed in the past.

Therefore, one of main factors causing the macro-economic problems is not over and has not been solved.

The Information Age technology changes will not be easily absorbed into our macro-economy without a strategic plan. We need to prepare to lessen the pressure of the _employment bubble_ caused by these technology changes.

Absorbing the pressure on the macro-economy will take

strategy and time. But, we don't have much time.

We have to skillfully act before the employment bubble causes a large burst in the corresponding macro-economy.

We need to keep the long-term wheel of supply, demand and workers rolling along for the macro-economy to also move forward.

When will technology's impact on the economy end? For the foreseeable future, the effect will continue as long as technology continues to advance.

Technology is advancing at an exponential-like pace now.

Technology can help us to reach great prosperity. A higher level of prosperity has never been seen before for so many. Yet, others are struggling to eat.

Technology is a double edged sword. Technology can be used for the betterment of all men, women and children. The ability to help all of our neighbors near and far, is within our hands.

Or, technology can lead to great destruction of others, ourselves, and our world.

Will technology be used for the benefit of mankind? Will there be a cure for cancer? Will there be a robot built little home for every homeless person? Will there be an abundance of organic food? Will there be pure and clean water?

Or, will technology be used to harm mankind? Will there be genetically modified organisms (GMOs) in foods that cause terrible diseases? Will there be a nuclear or a particle accelerator accident that devastates the world? (I am conCERNed!) Will there be World War III with unthinkable nuclear, chemical and/or biological destruction?

Some very educated people are concerned that technology could cause permanent harm to civilization.

"The Doomsday Clock is an internationally recognized design that conveys how close we are to destroying our civilization with dangerous technologies of our own making. First and foremost among these are nuclear weapons, but the dangers include climate-changing technologies, emerging biotechnologies, and cybertechnology that could inflict irrevocable harm, whether by intention, miscalculation, or by accident, to our way of life and to the planet."[14] (Emphasis added.)

I believe some solutions I suggest later in the book will help us to avoid destruction.

In the next chapter, I discuss how some economists are looking at our economic problems.

Then, I will discuss more about how the Federal Reserve and our government are dealing with the economy.

You might be surprised at what I add to the main causes of our economic crisis.

CHAPTER 2

ECONOMIC THEORIES ARE <u>NOT</u> CORRECTLY ANALYZING CRISIS

First, let's look at a little background of some of the people involved in analyzing the economy.

Robert Lucas, Jr. Ph.D. is a Professor Emeritus in Economics that won the 1995 Nobel Prize.[15]

The Library of Economics and Liberty website indicates, in pertinent part, the following information about Dr. Robert Lucas,

> "[Dr. Lucas'] major innovation in his seminal 1972 article was to get rid of the assumption (implicit and often explicit in virtually every previous macro model) that government policymakers could persistently <u>fool people.</u> Economists Milton Friedman and Edmund Phelps had pointed out that there should be no long-run trade-off between unemployment and inflation; or, in economists' jargon, that the long-run Philips Curve should be vertical.1 <u>They reasoned that the short-run trade-off existed because when the government increased the growth rate of the money supply, which increased prices,</u> **workers were fooled** <u>into accepting wages that appeared higher in real terms than they really were; they accepted jobs sooner than they otherwise would have, thus reducing unemployment</u>. Lucas took the next step by formalizing this thinking and extending it. He pointed out that in standard microeconomics, economists assume that people are rational. He extended that assumption to macroeconomics, assuming that people would

come to know the model of the economy that policymakers use; thus the term 'rational expectations.' This meant that if, say, the government increased the growth rate of the money supply to reduce unemployment, it would work only if the government increased money growth more than people expected, and the sure long-term effect would be higher inflation but not lower unemployment. In other words, the government would have to **act unpredictably**. . . .

One important implication of Lucas's work, which was confirmed by Thomas Sargent,2 is that a government that is credible—that is, a government that makes itself **understood and believed**—can quickly end a major inflation without a big increase in unemployment. The reason: government credibility will cause people to quickly adjust their expectations. The key to that **credibility**, wrote Sargent, is fiscal policy. If governments commit to balanced budgets, then one of their main motives for inflation is gone (see hyperinflation). . . .

In his Nobel lecture, . . . Lucas summed up his and others' contributions in the 1970s:
'The main finding that emerged from the research of the 1970s is that anticipated changes in money growth have very different effects from unanticipated changes. *Anticipated monetary expansions* have inflation tax effects and induce an inflation premium on nominal interest rates, but they are not associated with the kind of stimulus to employment and production that Hume described. *Unanticipated monetary expansions, on the other hand, can stimulate production as, symmetrically, unanticipated contractions can induce depression*.'3"[16]
(Emphasis added and reformatted.)

First, it is notable that Dr. Lucas understands that _fooling_ the people affects the economy and that _fooling_ the people can't persist. But, even if people could be continually fooled about monetary expansions, the fooling of the main population would not be the fully controlling issue in the long run.

Second, I disagree with the tunneled focus on the relationship of monetary policies and unemployment rates.

Third, fiscal and monetary policies BOTH must be credible to positively affect the economy.

Fourth, wages will not naturally increase as workers will not be needed because of technological advances. Regardless of the anticipated or unanticipated monetary expansions, technology will continue to cause increased unemployment. Because of the large supply of eager people seeking jobs even at lower wages, there will not be an inflationary push for higher wages.

Technological advances are the wall that the economy strategy will eventually have to either plan to navigate, crash into, or eliminate. Whether we see the wall or not, it is there. (Obviously, crashing would be terrible. Furthermore, even if some people wanted to halt all technological advances, elimination of all technological advances is impossible.) Whether people know about the monetary expansions or not, technology will take over more jobs and there will be more unemployment until there is some adjustment. For any U.S. economic strategy to be successful, the strategy must consider continued and future technological advances.

What unemployment percent is natural?

What unemployment rate should be the goal?

In an article entitled _Phillips Curve_, Kevin D. Hoover wrote in pertinent part,

"Most economists now accept a central tenet of both Friedman's and Phelps's analyses: there is some rate of unemployment that, if maintained, would be compatible with a stable rate of inflation. Many, however, call this the 'nonaccelerating inflation rate of unemployment' (NAIRU) because, unlike the term 'natural rate,' NAIRU does not suggest that an unemployment rate is socially optimal, unchanging, or impervious to policy. . . .

[T]he Congressional Budget Office estimated (Figure 3) that NAIRU was about 5.3 percent in 1950, that it rose steadily until peaking in 1978 at about 6.3 percent, and that it then fell steadily to about 5.2 by the end of the century. *Clearly, NAIRU is not constant. It varies with changes in so-called real factors affecting the supply of and demand for labor such as demographics, **technology,** union power, the structure of taxation, and relative prices (e.g., oil prices). NAIRU should not vary with monetary and fiscal policies, which affect aggregate demand without altering these **real factors**.*"[17] (Emphasis added and figures not included.)

Technology will be an exponentially increasing and leveraging factor on the unemployment rate.

There is no rate that would be natural. If left to the control of technology, the unemployment rate would increase until there is depression and social change.

Some people think that monetary policies alone prevent a depression.

According to a speech by Ben Bernanke, Bernanke was the Chairman of the Federal Reserve from 2006-2014.[18]

In Paul Krugman's interesting book entitled *The return of depression economics and the crisis of 2008*, Krugman wrote that Robert Lucas had claimed in 2003 that depression prevention was a solved problem.[19] Krugman added that, one year later, Ben Bernanke had also claimed that depression-prevention was a solved problem.[20]

Krugman wrote,

"Looking back from only a few years later, with much of the world in the throes of a financial and economic crisis all too reminiscent of the 1930s, these optimistic pronouncements sound almost incredibly smug."[21]

Krugman further elaborated that Ben Bernanke and Bob Lucas had both claimed that the economy would continue to exhibit some occasional downs, but there would not be any more severe recessions or a depression.[22]

From the severe economic crisis that occurred after their statements, we see that Ben Bernanke and Robert Lucas both were **devastatingly wrong**.

What do some economic theories suggest should be done in order to prevent recessions and depressions?

The two main economic theories are not correctly focusing on some of the biggest factors causing our U.S. macro-economic problems. The liberal Keynesian Theory and the conservative Supply-Side Theory are both wrong on how to handle our current macro-economy.

First, the Keynesian Theory focuses on decreased demand. Paul Krugman wrote,

"Whatever you do, don't say that the answer is obvious - that recessions occur because of X, where X is prejudice of your choice. The truth is

that if you think about it - especially if you understand and generally believe in the idea that markets usually manage to match supply and demand - recession is a very peculiar thing indeed. For during an economic slump, especially a severe one, supply seems to be everywhere and demand nowhere. There are _willing workers but not enough jobs_, perfectly good factories but not enough order, open shops but not enough customers. It's easy enough to see how there can be a shortfall of demand for _some_ goods; . . . . **But how can there be too little demand for goods in general? Don't people have to spend their money on something**?"[23] (Emphasis added.)

Here, Krugman discusses the lack of jobs, but he does not connect the lack of jobs with the transition into the Information Age. If people don't have jobs, they don't have money to spend. Krugman puts the cart before the horse.

Krugman compared a babysitting cooperative that eventually increased the supply of babysitting coupons, to the Federal Reserve increasing the money supply.[24] Krugman sees the problem as,

"Recessions, in other words, can be fought simply by printing money–and can sometimes (usually) be cured with surprising ease. . . .

[A] recession is normally a matter of the public as a whole trying to accumulate cash (or, what is the same thing, trying to save more than it invests) and can normally be cured simply by issuing more coupons.

The coupon issuers of the modern world are known as central banks: the Federal Reserve, the European Central Bank, the Bank of Japan, and so on. And it is their job to keep the economy on an even keel by adding or subtracting cash as needed."[25] (Emphasis added.)

Demand-side economists are missing the bigger picture. Superficially and temporarily attempting to artificially cause an overall change in demand by printing more money will not solve the problem.

For example, attempts to stimulate the economy with one-time government Stimulus Checks to the people will not permanently solve the economic problems of unemployment caused by the transition from the Industrial Age into the Information Age.

Likewise, temporarily increasing the money supply, lowering interest rates, monetizing the debt, etc., will not solve the root of the problem of unemployment.

In addition, people that have money will only spend it on what they need and what they want. People with a large amount of money only need and only want to buy a limited amount of products and services. People do not have to spend all of their money on something. How many cars and homes does a rich person want to buy? Some people will just continue to accumulate a lot of money.

People also do not base their shopping decisions based on what products employ the most people.   Think about it . . . Consumers generally do not even know how products are made. For example, even if a mass production of a product was made by one man pushing a single button to run a completely automated robotic manufacturing plant in the future, consumers would generally not know how the product was made.

Instead, people primarily consider the price and quality of the product they are buying.

Monetary and fiscal policies can also affect the unemployment rate. But, monetary and fiscal policies should consider the large impact that technological advances have on unemployment rates.

More, technology, freedom, monetary policies, and fiscal policies are all related. Indeed, if technology's affect on unemployment is not fully taken into consideration, the monetary, fiscal, and social health of our nation will suffer.

So, a main liberal economy theory is missing the bigger picture.

Now, let's look at a second economic theory.

Some conservative economists focus on balancing the budget and allowing the economy to self-adjust itself in a long painful process. In his 2011 book entitled *The Ten Trillion Dollar Gamble: The Coming Deficit Debacle and How to Invest Now*, Russ Koesterich wrote,

> "Since the 1980's, economists have periodically warned that the rising U.S. national debt was going to cause big problems for the United States. But in the past when they issued these warnings, they were talking about some time in the abstract future. We are now rapidly approaching that future. The government's continuing inability to balance its budget is about to move from the abstract to the concrete. The enormous U.S. deficit will soon fundamentally change the world's economic and financial climate: taxes will begin to rise, benefits levels will start to fall, and interest rates will go up. Furthermore, unless the United States' political class begins to demonstrate far more courage and resolve than it has in the past, inflation may jump as well."[26] (Emphasis added.)

Of course, I agree that inflation, taxes, benefits, and

interest rates are large concerns.

Koesterich also wrote,

"In 2002, former Vice President Dick Cheney famously remarked that 'Reagan proved that deficits don't matter.' Unfortunately, Cheney was wrong. Deficits do matter, and more importantly, they will eventually start impacting individual Americans. The fact that we've gotten away with our financial profligacy in the past does not mean that we will get away with it in the future."[27] (Emphasis added.)

I also agree that deficits do matter. Cheney was wrong. Deficits matter now and in the future for the next generation.

(As a side note: Sure, it would have been better if our country had moved toward planned solutions to the transition into the Information Age many years ago. If the U.S.A. would have done this, I strongly believe our current budget could have been balanced and we would have a much smaller amount of total U.S. debt.

Obviously, balancing the budget and reducing our U.S. debt are future goals, and it will take time to achieve these goals again. However, we have to deal with the situation we are in now.)

As I will discuss in a later chapter of this book, the huge debt now might also even have something to do with the world's view of the strength of the U.S. dollar, the IMF, and the World Bank. So, there is a credibility factor.

Koesterich stated,

"One place in particular in which the weak economy was felt was the labor market. Typically, when the economy is strong it creates more jobs.

28

You can explain more than 50 percent of the variation in labor market growth by changes in GDP. <u>When growth is weaker, job creation lags.</u>"[28] (Emphasis added.)

I strongly disagree with Koesterich on this point. Koesterich does not adequately address that in the transition into the Information Age, the GDP (Gross Domestic Production) could actually grow by using alternatives (computers, robotics, etc.) to human labor. **While the GDP could grow, some could grow rich while others could be jobless.** The overall macroeconomic result to the USA and world could likely be a recession/depression with devastation to many people. More production does not mean more jobs because technological advances such as robots can do the jobs.

Many Supply-Side economists are also missing the bigger picture for a solution. Superficially attempting to quickly cause an overall change in a country's macro-economy with a balanced budget and lower taxes will not solve the problem of the lack of jobs which is largely caused by the transition into the Information Age.

For example, attempts to quickly and completely balance the budget at this time will cause more unemployment and will not solve the problems. In addition, giving the wealthy and businesses *general* tax breaks will <u>not</u> solve the problem of the transition into the Information Age. (The key word here is "general" tax breaks.)

Many businesses are corporations that have a duty to their stockholders to maximize profits. Therefore, companies will simply take the profit earned and become more lean businesses. For example, if a manufacturer earned an increased profit with a general tax break, it may use the extra money to setup more robotics and terminate more "unnecessary" employees.

So, the solution is also not the conservative Supply-Side

Theory.

In addition, the solution is not a compromise between the Keynesians and the Supply-Siders. Both of these opposite positions do not solve the unemployment and macro-economy problems caused by the transition from the Industrial Age to the Information Age. A compromise of these two positions would also not correctly deal with the problems of unemployment caused by technology changes. Therefore, a compromise would also be ineffective.

Furthermore, vacillating back and forth over the years between the Keynesian Theory and the Supply-Side Theory will also be counter-productive and will not solve the important economic challenges caused by the transition from the Industrial Age to the Information Age. The government is not efficient and often makes no sense.

For example, the Federal government shutdown in Oct. 2013 resulted in Federal employees not working for 16 days.[29] The Federal employees then got back pay for the time of the government shutdown.[30] It was also reported that some Federal employees would likely get paid both unemployment compensation and back pay for not working during the Federal government shutdown.[31] This is an excellent example of the opposite economic theories not solving the problems, working against the other, and causing ridiculous results.

The solution is not the liberal Keynesian Theory or the conservative Supply-Side Theory.

Some will also argue that this Information Age step of technology is going to eventually bring about more jobs and a better macro-economy by itself. That would be great if it were true! However, I believe this is a terrible wrong assumption. This is also only wishful thinking.

In the future, there will be an even more decreased need for human labor because of technology. Of course, if people don't have jobs, they tend to have a lot less money to buy things or to pay for things they have purchased. We need to keep the long-term wheel of supply, demand and workers balanced. If the wheel of supply and demand is not balanced, the economy will have enormous difficulty rolling along and moving forward. We need solutions to deal with the negative effects to our macro-economy caused by changes in technology.

Obviously, the U.S. went with the liberal Demand-Side economics to attempt manage the U.S. economy and to resolve U.S. economic problems. So, more U.S. money was printed (and invisibly made with computers bytes and screens) and our U.S. debt climbed beyond most people's wildest imaginations.

Next, let's look at the huge U.S. debt.

CHAPTER 3

HUGE U.S. DEBT

How did the Federal Reserve deal with the recent economic problems? The Federal Reserve appears to have followed the Keynesian Theory.

The Federal Reserve flooded the market with low interest rates and with an increased supply of money.

The easy money was, and is, only a temporary shot in the arm to the economy. This shot was only a pain reliever and not a cure.

What happens when companies got the very low interest rates? With the very low interest rates, companies could afford to buy more new computers, robotics and other new technology. The new technology helped companies to make more products more efficiently and at a lower cost. There was also a general increase in potential gross national production (GDP).

But, who would buy the products from the companies?

Just like the Great Depression of the Industrial Age, the recent change into the Information Age technology step resulted in an overall decreased need for employees.

Therefore, in the recent Great Recession, we saw, and we will still see, high unemployment.

Did the Federal government correctly diagnose and deal with the technology changes affect on the macro-economy? No.

The root issue of the technology changes from the Information Age negatively affecting the unemployment rate which led to trouble in our macro-economy was <u>not</u> correctly diagnosed.

More, we saw the Federal government authorize bank bail-outs, automotive manufacturer bail-outs, etc. However, all the bailout money did not solve the problem of the lack of jobs.

The below chart and the below table show the total U.S. debt for the years ending 1999, 2004, 2009 and 2014, respectively.[32] The following chart and table show the large growth of total U.S. Debt.

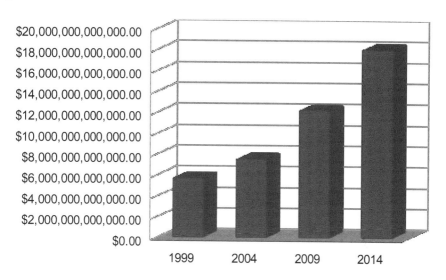

YEAR ENDING	U.S. DEBT
1999	$5,776,091,314,225.33
2004	$7,596,142,802,424.14
2009	$12,311,349,677,512.00
2014	$18,141,444,135,563.30

We know that the amount of debt is already huge.

The debt also increased rapidly.

In addition, the U.S. debt is still growing.

The U.S. debt has increased substantially. We can't just keep building up more government debt for use on the wrong solutions.

As you see in the above graph and table, I provide the U.S. debt on 5 year intervals.

As I was finishing this book, I went online to research a more recent U.S. debt. As of February 15, 2017, the U.S. debt was **$19,937,364,595,503.01**.[33]

Wow! That is almost **20 Trillion dollars!**

From what is being officially disclosed, the amount of U.S. debt has continued to rise to a ridiculous level.

The debt might even be worse than we know.

In any regard, we know it is huge.

People need to trust that the money they exchange has value. We just can't continue to incur an ever increasing debt.

More important, the large U.S. debt is not solving our long-term macro-economic problems.

Instead, many people are still unemployed and the U.S. debt has massively grown.

We need to quickly, properly and carefully act before the employment and debt bubble causes a large burst in the corresponding macro-economy.

Many people don't trust the government.

Who controls the money supply and interest rates? The Federal Reserve.

Who is controlling our monetary policy? The Federal Reserve.

Next, you will probably be surprised as I discuss: What is the Federal Reserve?

CHAPTER 4

FEDERAL RESERVE - ARE YOU FED UP?

Hold on tight, the Federal Reserve roller coaster might be a scary and bumpy ride . . .

Investopedia website states in pertinent part,

"What is a 'Central Bank'[?]

A central bank, or monetary authority, is a monopolized and often nationalized institution given privileged control over the production and distribution of money and credit. In modern economies, the central bank is responsible for the formulation of monetary policy and the regulation of member banks."[34] (Emphasis added.)

What is the central bank in the United States of America?

In the United States, the central bank is the Federal Reserve System (i.e., "the Fed") which was established by Congress' 1913 Federal Reserve Act."[35]

The word "Federal" in the Federal Reserve's name makes it sound like the Federal Reserve is part of the United States of America government. Most people might not know this, but the Federal Reserve is **not** part of the United States of America's government!

What is the Federal Reserve? The Federal Reserve's website stated,

"As the nation's central bank, the Federal Reserve derives its authority from the Congress of the United States. It is considered an **independent** central bank because its **monetary policy** decisions do ***not*** have to be approved by the President or anyone else in the executive or legislative branches of government, it does not receive funding appropriated by the Congress, and the terms of the members of the Board of Governors span multiple presidential and congressional terms. . . ."[36] (Emphasis added.)

Therefore, the Federal Reserve's decisions are even above the control of the elected President and elected Congress of the United States. Ridiculous!

Another page of the Federal Reserve website states in pertinent part,

"Who are the members of the Federal Reserve Board, and how are they selected?

The members of the Board of Governors are nominated by the President of the United States and confirmed by the U.S. Senate. By law, the appointments must yield a 'fair representation of the financial, agricultural, industrial, and commercial interests and geographical divisions of the country,' and no two Governors may come from the same Federal Reserve District.

The full term of a Governor is 14 years. . . .

Once appointed, **[the Federal Reserve's Board of] Governors may not be removed from office for their policy views**. The lengthy terms and staggered appointments are intended to contribute to the **insulation** of the Board--and the Federal Reserve System as a whole--from day-today political pressures to which it might otherwise be subject. . . ."[37] (Emphasis added.)

Why would the U.S. President nominate and the U.S. Senate confirm the Federal Reserve Board of Directors and then let them independently control the economy? This was a tremendous mistake.

Let's look at the Federal Reserve a little further. The Federal Reserve's website previously stated (but while I was recently writing this book the wording of the website was changed),

"Who owns the Federal Reserve?

The Federal Reserve System fulfills its public mission as an **independent** entity within government. It is not "owned" by anyone and is not a private, profit-making institution. . . .

The *12 regional Federal Reserve Banks*, which were established by the Congress as *the operating arms* of the nation's central banking system, are organized similarly to private corporations--possibly leading to some confusion about "ownership." For example, the Reserve Banks *issue shares of stock to member banks*. However, owning Reserve Bank stock is quite different from owning stock in a private company. The Reserve Banks are not operated for profit, and ownership of a certain amount of stock is, by law, a condition of membership in the System. The stock may not be sold, traded, or pledged as security for a loan; *dividends are, by law, 6 percent per year.*"[38] (Emphasis added.)

The Federal Reserve's website was changed and on October 18, 2016 I found the Federal Reserve website states,

"Who owns the Federal Reserve?

The Federal Reserve System is not "owned" by anyone. Although parts of the Federal Reserve System share some characteristics with private-sector entities, the Federal Reserve was established to serve the public interest.

The Federal Reserve derives its authority from the Congress, which created the System in 1913 with the enactment of the Federal Reserve Act. This central banking "system" has three important features: (1) a central governing board--the Federal Reserve Board of Governors; (2) a decentralized operating structure of 12 Federal Reserve Banks; and (3) *a blend of public and private characteristics*.

The Board of Governors in Washington, D.C., is an agency of the federal government. The Board--appointed by the President and confirmed by the Senate--provides general guidance for the Federal Reserve System and oversees the 12 Reserve Banks. The Board reports to and is directly accountable to the Congress but, unlike many other public agencies, it is not funded by congressional appropriations. In addition, though the Congress sets the goals for monetary policy, decisions of the Board--and the Fed's monetary policy-setting body, the Federal Open Market Committee--about how to reach those goals do not require approval by the President or anyone else in the executive or legislative branches of government.

Some observers mistakenly consider the Federal Reserve to be a private entity because the Reserve Banks are organized similarly to private corporations. For instance, each of the 12

Reserve Banks operates within its own particular geographic area, or District, of the United States, and each is separately incorporated and has its own board of directors. Commercial banks that are members of the Federal Reserve System hold stock in their District's Reserve Bank. However, owning Reserve Bank stock is quite different from owning stock in a private company. The Reserve Banks are not operated for profit, and ownership of a certain amount of stock is, by law, a condition of membership in the System. In fact, the Reserve Banks are required by law to transfer net earnings to the U.S. Treasury, **_after_** providing for all necessary expenses of the Reserve Banks, legally required dividend payments, and maintaining a limited balance in a surplus fund."[39] (Emphasis added.)

I agree that the Federal Reserve is serving the public interest - that is, I believe that the Federal Reserve is serving the public interest money over to the wealthy bankers.

The Federal Reserve Bank of St. Louis website has the following information in more plain English. The Federal Reserve Bank of St. Louis website states in pertinent part,

"Who Owns Reserve Banks?

On Dec. 23, 1913, President Woodrow Wilson signed the Federal Reserve Act. Over the next year, a selection committee made up of Secretary of the Treasury William McAdoo, Secretary of Agriculture David Houston, and Comptroller of the Currency John Williams decided which U.S. cities would be a place of residence for one of 12 Federal Reserve District Banks."[40] (Emphasis added and reformatted. Note: This paragraph is with an image appearing to be of a signing.)

44

Again, the text version download from the website of the Federal Reserve Bank of St. Louis states in pertinent part,

"Who Owns Reserve Banks?

The Federal Reserve Banks are not a part of the federal government, but they exist because of an act of Congress. Their purpose is to serve the public.

So is the Fed private or public?

The answer is both.

While the Board of Governors is an **independent** government agency, the Federal Reserve Banks are set up like **private corporations**. Member banks hold stock in the Federal Reserve Banks and earn dividends. Holding this stock does not carry with it the control and financial interest given to holders of common stock in for-profit organizations. The stock may not be sold or pledged as collateral for loans. **Member banks also appoint six of the nine members of each Bank's board of directors**."[41] (Emphasis added and reformatted.)

Is the Federal Reserve Board better able to handle our nation's economy than our government? **No. The Federal Reserve has been in charge of our nation's monetary policy for a very long time and our U.S. economy is in terrible shape.**

We often think that people are more intelligent and better able to handle matters because they were in appointed positions to make the decisions. This should not be presumed true. We need to research and make up our own minds about whether people in charge are able to handle matters. Look at all of the wrong things people in charge have done in history.

45

Although I don't consider the Federal Reserve to be part of our government (which I will explain more later), I trust no one in government to do the right thing. Obviously, our nation's Founding Fathers also did not trust people in governments. That is why our U.S. government was set up with a Constitution, and with checks and balances of powers. So, if we see mistakes being made by people elected in government, we can quickly get rid of tyrants and incompetents in government.

But again, I don't consider the Federal Reserve to be part of our government. They also consider themselves independent of our government. So, as smart as our Founding Fathers were, they did not think through every scenario to prevent problems.

The Federal Reserve's power over the United States' monetary policy has more control over U.S. citizens than the U.S. government. However, we don't directly elect the Federal Reserve's Board of Governors. In addition, our U.S. government does not have direct control of the Federal Reserve's Board of Governors. As you will see, again and again, these were and are, huge mistakes.

The Federal Reserve Central Bank's "insulation" from the political (i.e., voting) process does not make sense. The best way for government to control its monetary policy is by having elected leaders of our government controlling our monetary policy. In my opinion, there is no doubt, it would be much better to have our U.S. President and Congress responsible for U.S. monetary policy directly through our U.S. Treasury. We could at least get public records and oust those that we feel are not doing the correct U.S. monetary policies.

A Federal Reserve Press Release on the Federal Reserve's website states that there were changes to the dividends to member banks. The Federal Reserve website states in

46

pertinent part,

"Federal Reserve Press Release

Release Date: February 18, 2016

For release at 4:00 p.m. EST

The Federal Reserve Board on Thursday issued an interim final rule that amends Regulation I to implement provisions of the Fixing America's Surface Transportation (FAST) Act. The FAST Act reduced the dividend rate applicable to Reserve Bank depository institution stockholders with total assets of more than $10 billion (large member banks) to the **lesser of** 6 percent **or** the most recent 10-year Treasury auction rate prior to the dividend payment. The dividend rate for other member banks remains at 6 percent. Reserve Banks typically pay dividends to member banks in June and December each year.

The interim final rule also adjusts the treatment of accrued dividends when a Reserve Bank issues or cancels capital stock owned by a large member bank.

The interim final rule is effective upon publication in the Federal Register. The Board will accept comments on the interim final rule for 60 days after publication in the Federal Register."[42] (Emphasis added.)

This Interim rule sounds good, but it shows that the Federal Reserve Bank deposit institution big bank stockholders were making the 6%. (The percentage payment to the large banks changed after I began to write this book.) No bank should make any dividend percentage for owning stock in the Federal Reserve Bank. Regardless of the dividend percentage to the banks, the Federal Reserve is still serving the rich bankers/financial corporations and the Federal Reserve should be ended completely now.

The Federal Reserve System is not a profit-making entity itself. Likewise, the 12 regional banks are operating arms of the Federal Reserve that are not operated for the profit of the 12 regional banks. However, the Federal Reserve Board acts through its 12 operating arms in a banking system that makes profits for the member banks. After all, we all know that banks are in business for profits. Therefore, the Federal Reserve System is a profit making system for the member banks.

In addition, the 6% dividends are profit-making for the member banks. Requiring by law that member banks buy stock does not negate the fact that many banks are at least making 6% on their stock. The dividends paid to banks are just part of the banks' revenues.

Banks also make profits when the banks get funds at low rates (from the Federal Reserve related sources) and make loans at higher rates, etc. Banks make profits in many ways. Later in this book, you will see some more shocking ways that banks/financial institutions make profits/invest.

Banks should only be loaning money and providing banking services to the public to try to make a profit.

Banks also create money out of thin air because the Federal Reserve sets the reserve requirements for banks. When a bank is only required to keep a small reserve of the money it holds as deposits, it loans out money it really does not have in the bank. For a very simplistic example, a bank with $1,000,000,000 in customer deposits could loan out 10 times the deposits if the reserve requirement was only 10% (i.e., $10,000,000,000 of bank loans x 10% = $1,000,000,000 of customer deposit reserves required).

Private banks are "interested" in making profits. Giving

the Federal Reserve central bank system the ability to set interest rates and to control the money supply is like putting the fox in the hen house and locking the door.

So, how did the Federal Reserve Banking System get all this power?

Sometimes in U.S. history, the United States had no private central bank at all.

Let's briefly look at some history of banking in the United States.

In 1690, "Paper currency in the United States is born, issued by the Massachusetts Bay Colony to fund military expeditions. Other colonies quickly take up the practice of issuing paper notes."[43]

In 1739, "Benjamin Franklin takes on counterfeiting, using his Philadelphia printing firm to produce colonial notes with nature prints—unique raised patterns cast from actual leaves. This process adds an innovative and effective counterfeit deterrent to notes."[44]

In 1775, Continental Currency emerges.[45] "The phrase _'not worth a Continental'''_ is coined after the Continental Congress issues paper currency to finance the Revolutionary War, currency that quickly loses its value because of a lack of solid backing and the rise of counterfeiting."[46] (Emphasis added.)

What is one large reason that the early American colonists' Continental Congress currency money lost its value?

British were covertly counterfeiting the U.S. money during the Revolutionary War.[47]

Of course, the British counterfeiting of the U.S. money was the British's attempt to destabilize the new United States' ability to finance the Revolutionary War. Obviously, the British counterfeiting intentionally depreciated the value of the Continental Currency.

This United States' first private central bank was established in 1791.

The U.S. Mint government website provides in pertinent part that,

> "When the framers of the U.S. Constitution created a new government for their untried Republic, they realized the critical need for a respected monetary system. Soon after the Constitution's ratification, Secretary of the Treasury Alexander Hamilton personally prepared plans for a national Mint. On April 2, 1792, Congress passed The Coinage Act, which created the Mint and authorized construction of a Mint building in the nation's capitol, Philadelphia."[48] (Emphasis added.)

The www.history.com website provides in pertinent part that,

> "The Bank of the United States was established in **1791** to serve as a repository for federal funds and as the government's fiscal agent. Initially proposed by Alexander Hamilton, the **First Bank** was granted a twenty-year charter by Congress in spite of the opposition of the Jeffersonians to whom it represented the dominance of mercantile over agrarian interests and an unconstitutional use of federal power. The Bank, based in Philadelphia with branches in eight cities, conducted general commercial business as well as acting for the government. It was both well managed and profitable, but it won the enmity of entrepreneurs and state banks, who argued that

its fiscal caution was constraining economic development. <u>Others were troubled by the fact that two-thirds of the bank stock was held by</u> **British interests**. These critics, working with agrarian opponents of the bank, succeeded in preventing renewal of the charter in **1811**, and the First Bank went out of operation."[49] (Emphasis added.)

So, after much resistance to this central bank, the first central bank ended approx. twenty years after 1791.

I find it very ironic, that <u>shortly **after**</u> our Declaration of Independence in 1776 and the bloody Revolutionary War against the British, the United States had a central bank with a large majority of British interests.

(British people and the country England are now close allies of the United States of America. The issue I raise is <u>not</u> anti-British and is not against any other country. The issue is: Should foreign investors from <u>any</u> country have ever been (or be) any part of our nation's central bank? The answer is absolutely, "No!")

(This leads to another question that is beyond this book – Are the people who run the Federal Reserve patriots and only concerned about what is best for the U.S. citizens? If you haven't already guessed it, you will later read about some of the actions of the current central bank in the U.S.A. (i.e., the Federal Reserve) that show that it was also even involved with loans to foreign banks and corporations.)

Is the U.S. a **sovereign** nation? YES!

Wasn't the Revolutionary War of **1776** for our nation's <u>independence</u>? YES!

What do we celebrate on **July 4ᵗʰ** each year? All U.S. citizens should know that on July 4ᵗʰ each year we celebrate

INDEPENDENCE DAY!

What motivated foreign bankers to be involved in our U.S. central banking system? The answer is obvious and simple. The foreign banks made money by being involved in the central banking system.

Almost all Americans have heard of Thomas Jefferson. The whitehouse.gov website confirms that Thomas Jefferson was an American Founding Father, a spokesman for democracy, the principal author of the Declaration of Independence (1776), and the third President of the United States (1801–1809).[50]

Ellen Hodgson Brown, J.D., wrote an interesting book entitled, *The Web of Debt, The Shocking Truth About Our Money System and How We Can Break Free*.[51] Brown quoted Thomas Jefferson as saying,

> "The treasury, ***lacking confidence in the country***, delivered itself bound hand and foot to bold and bankrupt adventurers and bankers pretending to have money, whom it could have crushed at any moment."[52]

So, even Thomas Jefferson later regretted that the United States relied upon private central bankers for money.

As indicated above, in 1811, the first central bank ended.

Perhaps, coincidentally (but some might argue not coincidentally), in 1812, we had another war with the British.

The www.history.com website provides in pertinent part that,

> "Soon, however, problems associated with the financing of the War of 1812 led to a revival of interest in a central bank, and in **1816**, the

Second Bank of the United States was established, with functions very much like the first."[53] (Emphasis added.)

Andrew Jackson was a major general in the War of 1812 and Jackson became a national hero when he defeated the British at New Orleans.[54]

Andrew Jackson later became the 7th President of United States from 1829 to 1837.[55]

The Second Bank of the United States was a **private corporation** and virtually a Government-sponsored monopoly.[56]

President Jackson fought strongly against the central bankers in the U.S.[57] Brown wrote that President Andrew Jackson said in his veto of the Bank Renewal Bill,

"There are no necessary evils in government. Its evils exist only in its abuses. . . . Many of our rich men have not been content with equal protection and equal benefits, but have besought us to make them richer by act of Congress. . . . ***[W]e can at least take a stand against*** all new grants of monopolies and exclusive privileges, against any **prostitution of our Government** to the advancement of the few at the expense of the many. . . ."[58] (Emphasis added.)

Brown also wrote,

"Whether Congress had the right to issue paper money, Jackson said, was not clear; **but** [quoting President Andrew Jackson], '***If Congress has the right under the Constitution to issue paper money, it was given them to be used by themselves, not to be delegated to individuals or to corporations.***'"[59] (Emphasis added.)

Brown further quoted President Jackson as calling the central bank,

"[A] hydra-headed monster eating the flesh of the common man."[60]

Clearly, by not allowing a private central bank in the U.S., President Jackson was fighting for the rights of our U.S. government and of our U.S. citizens.

The whitehouse.gov website provides,

"'The bank,' Jackson told Martin Van Buren, 'is trying to kill me, but I will kill it!' Jackson, in vetoing the recharter bill, charged the Bank with_ undue economic privilege."[61] (Emphasis added.)

While Jackson might have done other things wrong as president, he did one thing very right for the citizens of the United States at risk to his own life. President Jackson ended the Second Central Bank.

According to the www.history.com website, President Jackson began to take all federal funds from the Second Central Bank in the U.S. in 1833 and the Second Central Bank's charter expired in 1836.[62]

Here is a little interesting side-story that I don't just want to put in an endnote:

President Jackson was the victim of a failed assassination attempt.[63]

The story of the failed assassination attempt is very exciting.

The history.com website provides that on Jan. 30, 1835, Jackson personally fought the assassin and the assassin's two guns both misfired.[64] The history.com website states that,

> "At the time, Jackson's Democrats and the Whigs were locked in battle over Jackson's attempt to dismantle the Bank of the United States."

Unfortunately, the writer of this history labeled our heroic president as paranoid.[65] Since someone did try to kill President Jackson, I don't think President Jackson was paranoid.

History.com states,

> "[Jackson's] vice president, Martin Van Buren, was also wary and thereafter carried two loaded pistols with him when visiting the Senate."[66]

Wow! Why hasn't the story of President Andrew Jackson become a blockbuster movie?

-------->>>

According to Ellen Hodgson Brown, our **only** U.S. president to ever reduce our national debt to zero and have a surplus was President Andrew Jackson.[67]

So what happened after President Jackson stopped the private central bank in the U.S.? Brown wrote,

> "Jackson had captured the popular imagination by playing on the distrust of big banks and foreign bankers; but in throwing out the national bank and its foreign controllers, he had thrown out Hamilton's baby with the bath water, leaving banks in unregulated chaos. There was now no national currency. Banks printed their own notes and simply had to be trusted to redeem them in specie (or gold bullion). When trust faltered, there

would be a run on the bank and the bank would generally wind up closing its doors."[68] (Emphasis added.)

According to whitehouse.gov, Abraham Lincoln became the 16th President of the Unites States in 1861.[69] Lincoln is one of my favorite presidents.

President Jackson and President Lincoln both fought the central banks. But, as Brown wrote, President Jackson and President Lincoln had different ideas of how to proceed with the future creation of money.[70]

Remember, President Jackson left the banking industry to become like the wild west. Banks made their own money, so there was a <u>variety</u> of money being used.

First, what were some of the obstacles that President Lincoln was facing? Of course, we know that President Lincoln was president during the terrible U.S. Civil War. President Lincoln also wrote the patriotic Gettysburg Address. In the Gettysburg Address, President Lincoln wrote in pertinent part these beautiful words,

> "[T]hat we here highly resolve these dead shall not have died in vain; that the nation, shall have a new birth of freedom, and *that government of the people by the people for the people*, <u>shall not perish from the earth</u>."[71] (Emphasis added.) (Please see Addendum D of this book for a full transcript of the Gettysburg Address.)

Brown wrote about some of the other huge and historic issues that President Lincoln was facing,

> "[Abraham Lincoln] had to deal with treason, insurrection, and national bankruptcy within the first days of taking office. Considering the powerful forces arrayed against him, his

56

achievements in the next four years were nothing short of phenomenal."[72]

Brown brilliantly pointed out that President Abraham Lincoln's government did the following remarkable and historic accomplishments,

"[B]uilt and equipped the largest army in the world, smashed the British-financed insurrection, abolished slavery, and freed four million slaves. Along the way, the country managed to become the greatest industrial giant the world had ever seen. The steel industry was launched, a continental railroad system was created, the Department of Agriculture was established, a new era of farm machinery and cheap tools was promoted, a system of free higher education was established through Land Grant College System, land development was encouraged by passage of a Homestead Act granting ownership privileges to settlers, major government support was provided to all branches of sciences, the Bureau of Mines was organized, government in the Western territories were established, the judicial system was reorganized, labor productivity increased by 50-70 percent, ..."[73]

Regarding U.S. central banking, what did President Lincoln do differently than President Jackson? Brown wrote,

"[President Abraham] Lincoln tapped into the same cornerstone that had gotten the impoverished colonists through the American Revolution and a long period of internal development before that: _he authorized the government to issue its own paper fiat money_."[74] (Emphasis added.)

The Merriam-Webster dictionary defines "FIAT MONEY"

as "money (as paper currency) not convertible into coin or specie of equivalent value."[75]

So, we know that President Lincoln handled the fight against central banking differently than President Jackson.

Here is the <u>key</u> question and point: What was this paper fiat money that the United States printed during President Abraham Lincoln's term? It was the Greenbacks.

President Lincoln authorized the U.S. government to do its own central banking by printing Greenbacks.

According to the U.S. Treasury website,

> "**July 17, 1861** - An Act of Congress ordered the issue of currency to help fund the Civil War. Known as ***greenbacks*, they were the first non-interest bearing notes created by the government**. . . .

> **August 29, 1861** - The first United States currency was separated and sealed by hand by two men and four women in the basement of the Treasury. The currency was in the form of $1 and $2 United States Notes.

> **November 13, 1861** - Secretary Chase received a letter from Rev. M.R. Watkinson that was instrumental in adding the motto [']In God We Trust['] to United State money. . . .

> **July 11, 1862** - An Act of Congress empowered the Secretary of the Treasury to purchase equipment and hire employees to engrave and print currency notes in the Department of the Treasury. This later became the Bureau of Engraving and Printing."[76] (Emphasis added.)

The Greenbacks are great! Why would anyone not want the U.S. to create its own Greenbacks?

A very strong foreword by Reed Simpson in Ellen Hodgson Brown's book describes a terrible opposition to the U.S. government doing its own banking and creating its own fiat money without a private central bank. This foreword in Brown's book included,

> "An editorial directed against <u>Lincoln's</u> **debt-free Greenbacks**, attributed to <u>The London Times</u>, said it all: *'If that mischievous financial policy which had its origin in the North American Republic during the late war in that country, should become indurated down to a fixture, then that <u>Government will furnish its own money without cost</u>.* **It will _pay off_ its debts and be without debt. It will become prosperous beyond precedent in the history of the civilized government of the world.** *The brains and wealth of all countries will go to North America. That government must be destroyed or it will destroy every monarchy on the globe.'"* [77] (Emphasis added.)

Unfortunately, besides the great government Greenbacks, there were still independent private banks creating their own money. Therefore, money was not uniform.

How was the uniformity of money issue solved? The U.S. Treasury government website states,

> "**February 25, 1863** - Congress passed the National Banking Act, establishing new national banks to create a <u>**uniform**</u> **national currency** and help fund the Civil War. The act also created the Office of the Comptroller of the Currency to regulate the national banking system. Senator John Sherman, future Secretary of the Treasury,

introduced the bill into the Senate first because it was feared the House would vote down the bill if it didn[']t already have Senate approval."[78] (Emphasis added.)

But, the uniformity of the private banks printing their own money still had the banks doing what the U.S. Treasury should have done all by itself – creating and printing money. The U.S. government can, and should, create and print **ALL** of its own money at no interest.

The U.S. Treasury government website also provides,

> "**April 14, 1865** - President Abraham Lincoln approved of Secretary Hugh McCulloch[']s plan to create an **anti-counterfeiting** unit within the Treasury, the United States Secret Service. It was one of Lincoln[']s last official acts.
>
> **April 14, 1865** - John Wilkes Booth assassinated President Lincoln at Ford[']s Theater. . . .
>
> **July 5, 1865** - The United States Secret Service began operating as an anti-counterfeiting unit within the Department of the Treasury. . . .
>
> **November 25, 1874** - The **Greenback Party** was founded in Indianapolis, Indiana. It opposed Treasury policies, **advocated the suppression of bank notes and the payment of the national debt in greenbacks**. . . .
>
> **November 6, 1876** - The Secret Service thwarted an attempt to rob President Lincoln[']s grave. The men who attempted to steal the body were planning to use it as a bargaining chip to get a counterfeiter out of prison.

March 3, 1877 - The Bureau of Engraving and Printing became the exclusive printer of U.S. currency. . . .

May 31, 1878 - An Act of Congress forbade further retirement of U.S. legal tender notes. Previously, the Secretary of the Treasury had been allowed to retire U.S. legal tender notes from circulation."[79]   (Emphasis added.)

As you see in history, the U.S. did not always use a private central bank. Obviously, our nation did not learn from the painful lessons of history. We have another private (i.e., not directly in the U.S. government) central bank that started in 1913.

"March 14, 1900 - The Gold Standard Act officially placed the United States on the gold standard.

September 6, 1901 - President William McKinley was shot twice in Buffalo, New York by anarchist Leon Czolgosz at the Pan-American Exposition. McKinley's death led to the Secret Service permanently protecting the president. McKinley died of his wounds on September 14, 1901 after appearing to be recovering for several days. . . .

December 23, 1913 - **President Wilson signed the Federal Reserve Act into law, creating a new central bank**."[80] (Emphasis added.)

President Wilson made a huge mistake creating the new Federal Reserve System. Afterward, President Wilson later seemed to have realized his own mistake of creating the new central bank.

According to the Liberty-Tree.ca website, President Wilson is attributed as saying the following in reference to signing the Federal Reserve Act,

"A great <u>industrial nation</u> is controlled by its <u>system of credit</u>. <u>Our system of credit is concentrated</u>. The **growth of the nation,** *therefore, and all our activities are <u>in the hands of a few men</u>.*
We have come to be one of the worst ruled, one of the most completely controlled and dominated governments in the civilized world. No longer a government by free opinion, no longer a government by conviction and the vote of the majority, but a government by the opinion and <u>duress of a small group of dominant men</u>."[81]
(Emphasis added. Also, this website stated the source of, "Attributed. In reference to signing the Federal Reserve Act in 1913. Most likely a compilation of 2 quotes from [Woodrow Wilson's] book The New Freedom, 1916.")

Evidently, President Wilson does appear to have regretted creating the Federal Reserve.

Another page of the Federal Reserve website asks and answers an important question about the duration of the Federal Reserve,

"Is the Federal Reserve Act going to expire?

No. The Federal Reserve Act of 1913--which established the Federal Reserve as the central bank of the United States--originally chartered the Federal Reserve Banks for <u>20 years</u>. But in the McFadden Act of 1927, the Congress rechartered the Federal Reserve Banks into perpetuity, and so there is currently <u>no 'expiration date'</u> or repeal date for the Federal Reserve."[82] (Emphasis added.)

Let's look at another U.S. President's courage and

battles. We'll briefly look at John F. Kennedy's battle in war and another battle in central banking.

According to whitehouse.gov,

"In 1943, when [John F. Kennedy's] PT boat was rammed and sunk by a Japanese destroyer, Kennedy, despite grave injuries, led the survivors through perilous waters to safety."[83]

After President John F. Kennedy's death, President Kennedy's daughter, Caroline Kennedy, wrote a very nice introduction to a later edition of her father's book, *Profiles of Courage*, that included,

"John F. Kennedy began his public service career as a PT-boat commander in the South Pacific in World War II. While on patrol on the night of August 2, 1943, the PT-109 was rammed by a Japanese destroyer, the *Amagiri*, and exploded into flames, throwing crew members into the burning water. Two were killed and one was burned so badly he couldn't swim. Clutching a strap of the injured man's life jacket *in his teeth*, Lieutenant Kennedy towed the wounded sailor to the nearest island, three miles away. For the next six days, with little food or water, the men hid, fearing they would be captured by the Japanese. Each evening, Kennedy swam through the shark-infested waters to other islands seeking help, until he was spotted by two Solomon Islanders, Eroni Kumana and Biuku Gasa. . . ."[84] (Emphasis added.)

Also, according to whitehouse.gov,

"In 1955, while recuperating from a back operation, [John F. Kennedy] wrote Profiles in Courage, which won the Pulitzer Prize in history."[85] (Emphasis added.)

As you see, John F. Kennedy (JFK) wrote about courage and he was also courageous.

According to whitehouse.gov,

"John F. Kennedy was the 35th President of the United States (1961-1963), the youngest man elected to the office."[86] (Emphasis added.)

In President Kennedy's Inaugural Address, he stated the famous instruction,

"Ask not what your country can do for you--ask what you can do for your country."[87]

Some people believe that President Kennedy attempted (through Presidential Executive Order 11110) to get back our U.S. independence from the Federal Reserve system and for the U.S. government to do its own central banking.

The American Presidency Project website provides,

"Executive Order 11110—Amendment of Executive Order No. 10289 as Amended, Relating to the Performance of Certain Functions Affecting the Department of the Treasury
June 4, 1963

By virtue of the authority vested in me by section 301 of title 3 of the United States Code, it is ordered as follows:
SECTION 1. Executive Order No. 10289 of September 19, 1951, as amended, is hereby further amended --

(a) By adding at the end of paragraph 1 thereof the following subparagraph (j):

"(j) The authority vested in the President by paragraph (b) of section 43 of the Act of May 12, 1933, as amended (31 U.S.C. 821 (b)), to *issue silver certificates* against any silver bullion, silver, or standard silver dollars in the Treasury not then held for redemption of any outstanding silver certificates, **to prescribe the denominations of such silver certificates**, and to coin standard silver dollars and subsidiary silver currency for their redemption," and

(b) By revoking subparagraphs (b) and (c) of paragraph 2 thereof.

SEC. 2. The amendment made by this Order shall not affect any act done, or any right accruing or accrued or any suit or proceeding had or commenced in any civil or criminal cause prior to the date of this Order but all such liabilities shall continue and may be enforced as if said amendments had not been made.

JOHN F. KENNEDY
THE WHITE HOUSE,
June 4, 1963

[APP Note: Executive Order 10289 referred to in this order was in fact issued on September 17, 1951. However the original published version of EO 11110 referred to September 19, 1951. APP practice is to try to reproduce the original published document even if it includes typos.]"[88] (Emphasis added.)

President John F. Kennedy 's Executive Order 11110 was using silver backed U.S. Treasury certificates which would have put some central banking directly back into our U.S. Government's own control. If President John F. Kennedy 's

Executive Order 11110 was fully used and continued to be used, the U.S. could have regained some of our nation's ability to do our own central banking.

However, shortly after Executive Order 11110, President Kennedy was assassinated. (I do not suggest any theories on why, or how, President Kennedy was killed. Any such theories are beyond the scope of this book.)

According to whitehouse.gov,

> "On <u>November 22, 1963</u>, when he was hardly past his first thousand days in office, JFK was assassinated in Dallas, Texas, becoming also the youngest President to die."[89] (Emphasis added.)

To many citizens, President Kennedy was a U.S. hero.

What happened to silver certificates? The U.S. Dept. of the Treasury's government website page on silver certificates states in pertinent part,

> "On <u>May 25, 1964</u>, the Secretary of the Treasury announced that <u>silver certificates could no longer be redeemed for silver dollars</u>. Subsequently, another Act of Congress dated June 24, 1967, provided that the certificates could be exchanged for silver bullion for a period of one year, until June 24, 1968. Those certificates, which remain outstanding, are still legal tender and can be spent just like a federal reserve note."[90] (Emphasis added.)

So here we are today, with a yo-yo history of central banking in the U.S.A.

As you know, in the past, patriots had wrestled with the private central bankers' attempts at controlling United States money and credit.

For more than 200 years, we seem to never have permanently learned anything about central banking.

Each time private central banking came up, it was like a renewed issue, but was never fully dealt with permanently.

Private central banking has repeatedly come back in the United States of America.

We did not learn from Presidents Jefferson, Jackson, Lincoln, or Kennedy.

Even now, few still know this truth about our country's struggle with central banks dating back to our founding fathers.

The Federal Reserve is not really part of our U.S. government. The Federal Reserve is only authorized by our Federal government.

We all continue to walk around with debtors' notes that we call U.S. dollars in our pockets.

We are all like people fooled into being slaves of the credit debt of the Federal Reserve.

Who prints money for the delivery to the Federal Reserve System today? We currently make the money for the Federal Reserve!

The website for the Bureau of Engraving and Printing, U.S. Department of the Treasury, states,

"The BEP [Bureau of Engraving and Printing, U.S. Department of the Treasury] prints billions of dollars - referred to as Federal Reserve notes - each year for delivery to the Federal Reserve System. U.S. currency is used as a medium of exchange and store of value around the world. According to the Federal Reserve, there is approximately $1.43 trillion worth of Federal Reserve notes in circulation."[91]

Again, the United States does <u>not</u> need the Federal Reserve to do our central banking for the government. Again, our U.S. government even prints our own money for the United States.

So the U.S. government is paying the Federal Reserve Banking System for money the U.S. government prints that is only backed by the confidence people have in the U.S. government!

The United States borrowing money from the Federal Reserve is like a new car manufacturer asking to rent cars from a car lot that has no inventory of cars. So, the car renter manufactures cars, warranties the cars, delivers cars to the car lot, and then rents cars. Does this seem right to you? I hope not!

The U.S. government doesn't need to rent money. The U.S. government <u>literally</u> <u>makes</u> money! Then, the U.S. government <u>pays</u> central bankers for the use of the money we make! Absurd!

Who backs the money of the Federal Reserve? The U.S. government.

Who is the U.S. government? The citizens of the U.S. government are the U.S. government.

Therefore, we, the citizens of the U.S.A. (i.e., we the people, we the U.S. government) back the money.

Now the Federal Reserve and the U.S. debt seems more of a problem, right!

So, why do we, citizens of the U.S.A., pay private bankers for our own money that we print? We have been fooled, conned and tricked!

Why don't people in the United States know the truth about the Federal Reserve Banking System?

I am not sure. I was fooled for a long time, too.

Brown wrote that,

> "The key to [the private banking clique's] success was that *they would control and manipulate the money system of a nation while letting it appear to be controlled by the government*.[92] (Emphasis added.)

Brown is right. The illusion of the government control is a big reason that the Federal Reserve had the ability to control our U.S. central banking with fiat paper money.

I think people innocently trust the word "Federal." The word "Federal" as part of the Federal Reserve sounds like it is directly part of our government.

Our lack of knowledge is the reason we are unaware that we do NOT need a private central bank in the U.S.A. People are not taught correctly about the Federal Reserve.

Many people don't want to believe that our U.S. government has been paying for something that our nation has the sovereign right to do all by itself.

Most people are busy with their daily lives and work, and this is not in their area of interest. They trust the government will be looking out for their interests.

Why doesn't our government do something about our enormous and growing debt, debt interest, and private central bank? Many of our politicians like the money and don't understand the full paradigm.

Dr. Ron Paul served many terms in the U.S. House of Representatives and is a medical professional.[93] Dr. Ron Paul wrote an absorbing book entitled, *END THE FED*."[94]

Ron Paul wrote about a reason politicians don't challenge the Federal Reserve. Paul wrote,

> "***The fact that the [Federal Reserve] accommodates politicians is a good reason few challenge the Fed's authority. Spending gets members of Congress reelected*** by providing the goodies that constituents have become dependent on. There are limits on how much taxation the people will tolerate and how much the government can borrow without forcing up interest rates. The convenience of the Federal Reserve monetizing the debt satisfies a lot of people-until the day comes that we suffer the consequences with an economic downturn and higher prices.
>
> Higher prices represent a depreciation of the value of the dollar and are a tax on the people. The tax is borne by the middle class and the poor. ***The early users of the money are the beneficiaries; the government, the banks, and the large corporations.***
>
> This is a deceitful, unfair, and corrupt system. Not only does it transfer wealth from the middle class to the rich, it can postpone payments to the next generation just as borrowing does. . . .
>
> This is the plan: massive debt and inflation to ***bail out*** friends, pretending to prop up the economy and liquidate debt. It never goes as planned. . . ."[95] (Emphasis added.)

Dr. Paul has a good point. The <u>politicians don't want to</u> challenge the Federal Reserve because the Federal Reserve accommodates their big spending debt.

If people do want to research the issue, by the time we get to the third level of the Federal Reserve System's structure, most people are confused, lose interest, or don't have the time to do more research on the Federal Reserve.

Researching the Federal Reserve is not fun for everyone. Researching the Federal Reserve is like trying to find the center of an onion. If someone peels off one layer of onion, they find more and more layers. On the other hand, if someone cuts through the onion, they might feel like they are going to cry. Crying might be how you feel when you research the Federal Reserve and learn the truth.

Also, the debt is just growing and it does not seem real.

Even though the U.S. debt interest is a large burden on the back of the U.S., our lives have still been pretty good in the U.S. because of the innovation, technology and hard work of the U.S. citizens. In addition, our nation's abundant natural resources provide value to our U.S. currency. The U.S. dollar has also had the value benefit of being the world's favored reserve currency which provides purchasing power.

Furthermore, the Constitutional rights of citizens of the United States provide value to the U.S. currency. People want freedom. United States citizens still have a lot of freedom. Therefore, people want to be citizens of the United States. Our U.S. liberties provide large value to our U.S. currency.

People are smart in the U.S.A. The U.S. liberties and education provide us with questions:
Why did the economy go into a depression, a deep recession, etc.?
Why aren't there enough jobs?
Why is the U.S. debt so high?

Why do U.S. citizens have to pay high interest rates on homes when banks are provided bailouts and banks are provided with basically interest-free money?

How do we prevent another bad economic crash?

Will our U.S. economy collapse?

Earlier in this book, I said that you might be surprised at what I add to the causes of our economic problems. So, now you know, <u>the Federal Reserve is one of the major causes of our economic problems</u>.

All hope is not lost. We do not need a private central bank like the Federal Reserve.

We can get rid of the Federal Reserve.

Instead of the Federal Reserve, the U.S. government can print its own money, set its own interest rates, make its own credit, and make its own loans. We can turn the U.S. economy around.

People are waking up: The United States does <u>not</u> need the Federal Reserve or any other private central bank to loan money to the United States.

If we get rid of the Federal Reserve central banking system, what type of central bank entity should be in our sovereign United States of America?

As I wrote, our U.S. government's central bank should immediately be a direct part of our U.S. government.

Someone might argue, "But, Congress can't even handle a fiscal budget without shutting down the government." I would say this is correct. Change it. You are the government.

Someone might say, "The Federal government's policy is out of control." Again, I would say this is correct. Change it. You are the government.

Another person might argue, "Our U.S. government can't balance the fiscal budget and we are in too much U.S. debt." Correct. Change it. You are the government.

Would a central bank that is really part of the U.S. government be better than the Federal Reserve? Absolutely, YES!

If the government officials mess up our monetary policy (instead of the Federal Reserve messing up our monetary policy more), at least we can vote out terrible elected officials right away. Therefore, I would rather have our U.S. government handling our central banking system any day.

How should the central banking be structured within the U.S. government?

Really, this is a question of our type of government. We have a republic type of government - of the people, by the people, for the people - with a Constitution.

We are citizens in a sovereign nation. We are free! We are free to make our own laws! Our elected officials made laws for a private central bank. We can change those laws, now.

The citizens of the United States participating in our U.S. government, the real free press (news) reporting on our U.S. government's central bank, the checks and balances of our 3 branches of government, and the judiciary should be the constraints on the unlimited power of the Federal government to create its own money.

How would a government central bank be different from the private Federal Reserve Banking System?

The U.S. government can just create its own money at _zero interest_.

Again, the United States' central bank is an extremely important monetary system that has huge power over the citizens of the United States of America. Our directly elected officials in the U.S. government should control our nation's money supply, base interest rates, etc.

Money is a huge leverage of social control and social engineering. Money can influence government, politics, technology, education, versions of history, medicine, food and almost everything.

Unchecked, a private or government central bank's power could be extremely powerful and tyrannical.

How does our U.S. government make the changes to central banking in the U.S.A.?

Only some of our most trusted, loyal, patriotic government leaders opened their mouths once they saw the real problems of our private central bank. More, when some of our patriotic leaders became keenly aware of the problems of the central bank, it was still difficult to explain to the citizens of the U.S.A. and very difficult to make changes.

Brown's book includes a foreword by a banker and developer, Reed Simpson, M.Sc. Simpson's foreword in Brown's book stated,

> "Henry Ford said it best: *'It is well that people of the nation do not understand our banking and monetary system, for if they did, I believe there would be a revolution before tomorrow morning.'*"[96]

Violent revolution is not the answer to the how to get rid of the Federal Reserve.

In his book, Ron Paul stated,

"Most people, especially those in Washington, <u>still</u>
<u>believe this system can be salvaged. They are</u>
<u>wrong, and dangerously wrong</u>. We should work
for reform and sound economics with a strict
adherence to the Constitution, but, absent such
change, we should be prepared for
hyperinflation and a great deal of poverty with
a <u>depression and possibly street violence as</u>
<u>well</u>. The worse the problem, the greater the
chance a <u>war</u> will erupt, especially as
protectionist sentiments around the world
grow. These are the <u>wages of</u> <u>central</u>
<u>banking</u>."[97] (Emphasis added.)

Wow. Slow down everyone. Think about what Ron Paul
said. We must <u>not</u> agree to the costs of private of central
banking being hyperinflation, widespread poverty, depression,
street violence and war.

Some people might look at our nation as a board game.
We must consider that there might be some that would like to
tip over the board game and start the government over with
them in charge of central banking again. We must be alert to
potential manipulations.

War is not the answer to our Federal debt and central
banking crisis.

At the same time, I believe we must have a strong
national defense. If we don't have a strong U.S. national
defense, we will be at the mercy of any evil nation.

More, we must stand as an example of liberty to the rest
of the world. As an example of liberty, we will continue to have
the admiration of many people in foreign governments.

Instead of waging war, we need to always strive to
understand the relationships of technology, job wages, private
central banking and economies.

Ron Paul also wrote,

"Over the years, I have heard many businesspeople praise big government, saying how city hall and business must work together. It's a partnership that develops at all levels--city, state, federal, and international (UN, World Bank, IMF, and the multinational development banks). This is all done in the name of capitalism and financed by a **corrupt and complacent Federal Reserve money machine**. Home builders, highway contractors, bridge builders, and on and on, all support big government projects.

The sad part, when graft, corruption, and financial crisis results, is what gets blamed. Usually it's the free market, and the problems become an excuse to further inflate and enlarge the government while undermining the free market, always serving the special interests.[98] (Emphasis added)

Ron Paul wrote on how the powerful are getting money, but should have been allowed to go bankrupt,

"And yet someone is getting the money. Mostly it is powerful players in the market, institutions that are regarded as essential to national well-being, such as Goldman Sachs and AIG insurance. In fact, these companies could have been allowed to go bankrupt with no downside for the general population, just like Lehman Brothers was allowed to die. Yes, there would be pain, but at least it would be temporary. The current path is prolonging and extending the pain-while slow death dressed up in fancy clothes."[99](Emphasis added.)

I agree with Ron Paul on this point. No company should

have been found too big to fail. If the big players were allowed to fall, it would have been the best thing for the U.S. government and for the people. Change would have been the result.

I see the Federal Reserve and bankers/financial corporations as reaping the fruits of the profit that the freedom, hard work, natural resources, and the technology of the United States has produced. The Federal Reserve is then sliding the profits over to the families and friends of Federal Reserve and the crony government leaders.

Ron Paul also wrote,

> **"Law permits this highly <u>secretive</u>, <u>private</u> bank to <u>create credit</u> at will and distribute it as it sees fit.** *The chairman of the Federal Reserve can blatantly inject in a public hearing that he has no intention of revealing where the newly created credit goes and who benefits.* When asked, he essentially answered, **"It's none of your business," saying that it would be "counterproductive" to do so.** The entire operation of the Fed is based on an immoral principle. Congress contributes to the immorality by permitting the process to continue <u>without</u> <u>any true oversight</u>. The immorality associated with money is as much about omission as commission, Members of Congress, when they knowingly endorse this system of **_fraud_** because of the benefits they receive, commit an immoral act. Financing spending in an irresponsible manner, through Fed action or future debt burdens, provides immediate political benefits to politicians."[100] (Emphasis added.)

Again, I agree with Ron Paul. The operation of the Federal Reserve is secretive and immoral. We need change that prevents the government and the Federal Reserve from secretly doing things that will collapse our economy.

Ron Paul puts fault on the Federal Reserve and calls for the Federal Reserve to be abolished,

> "Unfortunately, since the housing bubble burst, signaling the end of a monetary era, everything Congress and the Fed have done has set the stage for a dollar crisis. That's very bad news since the rejection of the dollar will create, <u>mainly out of fear and a lack of any other ideas</u>, an even greater crisis than the collapse of the international financial system. ***The evidence is abundant that the Fed is at fault and should be <u>abolished</u>. So far, though, all Congress has done is give it even more power as the principal central economic planner.***"[101] (Emphasis added.)

I fully agree with Ron Paul that the Federal Reserve should be abolished.

Do we have a government of the citizens of the U.S.A., by the citizens of the U.S.A., and for the citizens of the U.S.A.?

Or, do we now have an oligarchy government instead of a republic government?

According to the online dictionary.com, one definition of "ol-i-gar-chy" is,.

> "1. a form of government in which all power is vested in a few persons or in a dominant class or clique; government by the few."[102]

We often think that power in the U.S. is in the hands of all of the U.S. citizens. With an oligarchy, the power is in a small number of people's hands.

In July 2015, former President Jimmy Carter discussed money and politics in an interview, and on the topic of underlined campaign financing,

>"Carter told Thom Hartmann . . . that, '[I]t violates the essence of what made America a great country in its political system.'"[103] (Emphasis added.)

In addition, in this interview former President Carter said,

>"*Now it's just an* **oligarchy**, *with unlimited political bribery* being the essence of getting the nominations for president or to elect the President."[104] (Emphasis added.)

In this interview, former President Carter also said,

>"And the same thing applies to governors and U.S. senators and congress members."[105] (Emphasis added.)

Think of the money involved with the Federal Reserve. Now, think of the power of the people involved with the Federal Reserve.

The Federal Reserve and its cronies are an oligarchy.

More, the Federal Reserve is an oligarchy that supports political and other oligarchies.

How do we make changes to central banking if there is an oligarchy?

As a sovereign nation, we are able to make our own laws, to print our own money, and do our own country's central banking! We just need to know that we can do these things. We are already free! We can vote and we have a Constitution. We have power by voting and talking. Again, we should not be fooled into a violent revolution.

Our U.S. government politicians and citizens need to understand that our government does not need to borrow money from banks.

We need to talk with each other. We need to write to politicians and newspapers. We need to communicate.

We need to become politically active. We must wake-up and participate in our government.

We need to prevent oligarchies. I firmly believe in the Declaration of Independence and our U.S. Constitution as the way to stop and prevent oligarchies in the U.S.A.

Governments can be extremely powerful and tyrannical.

Money is also a huge power.

Putting such powerful decisions into <u>non-elected</u> and <u>highly independent</u> Federal Reserve Board members' hands is not part of the Republic form of government that we all pledge our allegiance. A United States of America government website provides that our nation's *Pledge of Allegiance to the Flag* is as follows,

> "I PLEDGE ALLEGIANCE TO THE FLAG OF THE UNITED STATES OF AMERICA AND **TO THE REPUBLIC** FOR WHICH IT STANDS, ONE NATION UNDER GOD, INDIVISIBLE, WITH LIBERTY AND JUSTICE FOR ALL."[106] (Emphasis added.)

We are supposed to elect people in a Republic form of government.

The U.S. government can fully be, and should fully be, its own central bank.

History shows us that laws on central banking in the U.S. have gone back and forth with only temporary solutions.

We could change central banking in the U.S. with laws again. But, as you know, those changes could be very temporary, and a private central bank could pop up its head again in the U.S.

We need a permanent stop of, and prevention of, private central banking in the U.S.

Therefore, we need an **amendment** to our U.S. Constitution regarding central banking.

The problem with the Federal Reserve is that it is <u>not</u> directly a part of our government.

Therefore, I believe that our U.S. government should make its own central bank that is a direct part of the U.S. government.

What type of money should our U.S. government's own central bank create?

I believe that the U.S. government should create its own fiat money.

We have been using fiat money in the U.S. for a long time. We should continue to use fiat money.

The monetary policies that the U.S. Government Central Bank sets should be 100% for the benefits of the U.S. citizens. Making money and managing the money supply is not expensive. Our government should be able to create money at almost no cost. More, it would cost the U.S. government 0% interest to make its own money. Then, our government can make money by loaning money at higher interest rates to banks.

Others disagree.

Everyone knows that money doesn't grow on trees. Ron Paul emphasizes the point and goes further when he states,

> **"It's as if we still believe that money can be grown on trees, and we don't stop to realize that if it did grow on trees, <u>it would take on the value of leaves in the fall, to be either mulched or bagged and put in a landfill. That is to say, it would be worthless</u>**. Why bright people in an advanced society can conclude that wealth can be increased by merely expanding the money supply is bewildering. I suspect that those who are the real promoters of central banking and <u>fiat money</u> are more motivated by power and greed than they are by sound economic theory. **Many others are complacent and trusting and have probably not thought the issue through.**"[107] (Emphasis added.)

Fiat money can be worthless sometimes. But, in the U.S.A., our Constitution, freedoms, liberty, values, stability, social safety, military, and production make the Federal Reserve's fiat money strong.

Paul wrote,

> "In an ideal world, the Fed would be abolished forthwith and the money stock frozen in place. . . . Congress would remove the Fed's charter. . . . [T]he dollar would be reformed so that it again would become <u>redeemable in gold</u>. The federal government's gold stock could be used to guarantee convertibility at home and abroad. All remaining powers associated with money could then be transferred to the U.S. Treasury, but now there would be a check on what government did

with its power."[108] (Emphasis added.)

I understand Paul's reasoning, but I disagree with Paul's suggestions on gold. If we transfer money to a gold standard now, people would immediately redeem all the gold to the point of busting our currency. Obviously, it is too late, there is too much money in the U.S. currency, and there is not enough gold

In addition, I don't feel that our nation could take the shock of converting to a non-fiat currency now.

(Maybe, 25 years in the future, after our national economic crisis is stabilized and *if* the government's own central bank fiat system is not working well, a gold standard (or better, other precious metals/other commodities standard) currency could be implemented in the U.S.A. Hopefully, this will not be needed.)

Another reason I don't want a gold standard now is that the wealth of the world has already been moved from the common people to the wealthy. Gold has already been purchased so that the wealth would still be in the hands of the people that are already wealthy. Most people only hold paper (fiat) money now. So, if a gold standard would have been better, it is too late for it now.

The value of money is not primarily whether it is paper or gold.

What really makes paper or gold valuable?

For many things, something is valuable when people put a value on it and want it.

If almost all people put value on U.S. fiat dollars that the U.S. prints when doing its own central banking without the Federal Reserve, then it will have value.

As you know, the Federal Reserve is currently using fiat money. The U.S. fiat currency from the Federal Reserve worked and was valued for a long time because it was the U.S. currency (but, it was unnecessarily costing our nation a lot of money because it was not really created through our government). Therefore, the fiat money created directly from the U.S. government without the Federal Reserve will eventually be even stronger than the present Federal Reserve's fiat money.

Again, people value our U.S. fiat currency because of unique factors found in the U.S.A. For example, people value our U.S. currency because of our government stability, national production, national resources, safety, military, amount of debt, etc. In addition, people in the world value our U.S. currency because of our type of government (i.e., a Constitutional Republic) and our freedoms.

If we change to a gold standard of U.S. currency now, people might just view our U.S. currency as a gold commodity. This will cause people to compare and value our U.S. currency based on other gold in the world. People will probably not give such U.S. gold-backed currency its full value based upon the unique factors found in the U.S.A.

More important, if the U.S. went to a gold standard currency now, it would be extremely expensive and difficult for our U.S. government to create and maintain.

On the other hand, if the U.S. printed its own paper (fiat) money through its own real government central bank, it would take very little resources (e.g., paper) and it would be very easy for the U.S. to continue to print currency.

Therefore, even if a gold standard U.S. currency had some benefits, it would not be fair or prudent for the U.S. to change to a gold currency now.

In *Money: How the Destruction of the Dollar Threatens*

the Global Economy-- and What We Can Do About It, Steve Forbes and Elisabeth Ames wrote about the crisis of modern economies and money.[109]

I disagree with Forbes and Ames from the beginning. In the book's opening, it says,

> "In remembrance of Alexander Hamilton, our first Secretary of the Treasury, who established a financial system that propelled generations of entrepreneurs and made America the most creative country on earth. *Like few others before or since, he showed that money, properly understood, is the root of all good.*"[110] (Emphasis added.)

> Money is not the root of all good.

> "For the love of money is the root of all evil: which while some coveted after, they have erred from the faith, and pierced themselves through with many sorrows." 1 Timothy 6:10 King James Version (KJV) Holy Bible[111] (Emphasis added.)

Forbes and Ames also make a proposal for a new U.S. gold standard currency.[112] Again, I disagree with the idea of moving back to a gold standard now. In my opinion, a terrible part of Forbes' and Ames' proposal is that it would not immediately end the Federal Reserve. Forbes/Ames writes,

> "The Fed would continue to act as a lender of last resort and deal with panics that might arise from a 911 type of event."[113]

I do not want to keep the Federal Reserve at all. I suggest that the U.S. government immediately and completely abolish the Federal Reserve.

The Federal Reserve and the Federal government already drove the U.S. economy off the cliff. But, we can survive and thrive if we use some more U.S. innovation. I will provide a summary of some of my suggested solutions later. But, we need more suggestions and a very open dialogue about the U.S. economy now.

Dr. Paul wrote,

"The entire system of fiat money and factional-reserve banking is a super-Ponzi-like scheme (if we can't pay it back, let's just create more!) and is the source of our problems."[114]

I see the Federal Reserve as a Ponzi-like scheme or other type of scam, too. I also see it as a huge illusion trick.

But I don't have the same concerns that Ron Paul does about fiat money.

Again, we have fiat money now and I don't see us being able to go to the gold standard without a lot of trouble and expense.

What is the main problem with the fiat money we have now? The U.S. fiat money is out of control and run by the Federal Reserve.

I do want the government to be its own central banker. The U.S. government should be the only central bank for the U.S. government.

Dr. Paul states,

"An end to the money-creating power and a transfer of remaining oversight authority from the Fed to the Treasury would be marvelous steps in the right direction. But let us stretch these ideas a bit further and reconsider the entire idea of a government monopoly on money. **The Founding Fathers never set out to create a single national monetary system. Money and banking were left to the states, with the proviso that the states themselves could <u>only</u> make gold and silver legal tender.** <u>At the same time, there were no restrictions on</u> **private minters and private (free) banking.** <u>We should embrace this system again,</u> **repealing legal tender laws and letting everyone get into the business of the production of money.** This would create a competitive market in which the best monies would emerge over time to compete directly with the federal government's dollar."[115] (Emphasis added.)

The founding fathers created our nation so that states could <u>only</u> make gold and silver legal tender coins. (See Article I, Section 10, of the *U.S. Constitution* in Addendum B.) The ability to make gold and silver coins is different than the ability to do central banking.

I believe the success of a real U.S. government central bank would greatly depend on whether people had confidence in it. As such, this might depend on whether a real U.S. government central bank would be responsible, fully transparent, etc. More, this also might depend on whether the Federal government was maintaining a balanced budget. In addition, it would depend on whether the Federal government required a real U.S. government central bank's fiat currency to be considered <u>legal tender</u>. The U.S. government would need to make it <u>mandatory</u> for a real U.S. government central bank's fiat money to be accepted as payment of all debts and purchases in order for the fiat money to work well. More, the Federal government would need to steadfastly defend against counterfeiting.

I also disagree with Dr. Paul about the idea of letting everyone into the business of making money. We should not have private minters and private bankers <u>creating</u> money. Having everyone create money would cause instability and chaos.

When you go to a store, you and the merchant need to have a meeting of the minds on price. How are you going to set a price with multiple private types of money being produced and utilized? This would be very difficult.

The price of the transaction would increase because of the need to take time to calculate, value and authenticate the different types of money. The transactions would also result in more disputes on the types of money.

How would you stop counterfeiters of privately minted money? This would also be very difficult.

Sales would drastically decline because of the price, disputes and delays in transactions.

Since sales would decline, there would also be a decreased need for production.

Jobs would follow sales and production, and more people would be unemployed.

This could lead to more economic crisis.

We want businesses and transactions to flourish. We want people to sell their goods quickly and easily. We need a standard currency in the United States. We don't want private corporate money to compete with U.S. government's dollars as the standard currency.

We already have bartering in the U.S. For example, person A might trade a car for a camper from person B. This might work for rare circumstances, but bartering is slow and cumbersome for daily business.

The fiat currency of the Federal Reserve worked for years, so I believe the fiat currency of a real Federal government's own direct central bank would work the same way (but, be better because it would be without the private Federal Reserve bank's interest rates and other costs). More, the real Federal government's own direct central bank would also work _better_ because it would be with full accountability, open records, full transparency, checks and balances, limited powers, etc.

Brown wrote,

"[A]ll it needed was a monetary medium that would allow this wealth to flow freely, circulating from the government to the people and back again, without being perpetually siphoned off into the private coffers of the bankers."[116]

A good monetary medium that would not siphon off interest on our government's monetary supply makes great sense. Again, this is one of the reasons that I believe the U.S. government should directly do its own central banking as part of the government.

I believe that U.S. government's fiat money is the best alternative at this time. However, a monetary medium (i.e., fiat money) is _not all_ that is needed.

We need a great government that is responsive to its people. We have a great framework for our government, but we need some changes.

Also, it would still be fine for small private banks to receive deposits and make loans. But, banks should not do other risky financial activities. (We will discuss this more in the next chapter.)

Can our government constitutionally do its own central banking directly as part of our U.S. government? Of course, yes!

Our U.S. government is a self-government. We are the government. We decide what our government can do.

Our U.S. self-government has many treasures. One of our treasures of our self-government nation is our nation's ability to do its own central banking. Our own U.S. government could, and should, directly create and print money at zero interest cost to our U.S. government.

The ***Declaration of Independence*** of the United States of America states,

> **"We hold these truths to be self-evident, *that all men are created equal, that they are endowed by their <u>Creator</u> with certain unalienable Rights, that among these are Life, Liberty and the pursuit of Happiness.--That <u>to secure these rights, Governments are instituted among Men, deriving their just powers from the consent of the governed</u>*. . . ."** [117] (Emphasis added.) (The U.S. Declaration of Independence is so important that I have included a transcript of it in Addendum A of this book.)

To "secure these rights," . . . think about those words. Our government was made to secure our rights.

"[Deriving their just powers from the consent of the governed." Again, think about these words. Our government gets its "just powers" from the "consent" of the citizens.

Looking more at these important words in our Declaration of Independence, we also see the basis our United States government is that God has <u>created</u> us, that we are <u>all equal</u>, that we have individual rights of "Life, Liberty and the pursuit of Happiness" in the United States, and that we have

90

the right of self-government. <u>If we have the right of self-government, then we decide our laws, not the bankers</u>. If we have the right of liberty, then we are not slaves. The Declaration of Independence did not cite to other legal authority. Rather, the Declaration of Independence clearly held these truths to be <u>self-evident.</u>

We do <u>not</u> need a private central bank to make money for the United States government. Again, we have <u>self-government</u>.

No doubt, the signers of the Declaration of Independence were risking their lives in the revolution.

The U.S. government derives its powers from the consent of the U.S. citizens under God, the Creator. We, the citizens, are the government under God.

More, think of the important words of the **_U.S. Constitution_**,

> "'**_We the People_** _of the United States_**, in Order to form a more perfect Union, establish Justice, insure domestic Tranquility, provide for the common defence, promote the general Welfare, and secure the Blessings of Liberty to ourselves and our Posterity, do ordain and **_establish_** _this Constitution for the United States of America_. . . ."[118] (Emphasis added. Also, see Addendum B in this book for a transcript of the Constitution.)

These are important words that men fought and died to create and preserve for our U.S. government. After the successful revolution, a Constitution was proposed.

The online Library of Congress website provides,

"The Federalist, commonly referred to as the

Federalist Papers, is a series of 85 essays written by Alexander Hamilton, John Jay, and James Madison between October 1787 and May 1788. The essays were published anonymously, under the pen name 'Publius,' in various New York state newspapers of the time.

The Federalist Papers were **written and published to urge New Yorkers to ratify the proposed United States Constitution**, which was drafted in Philadelphia in the summer of 1787. . . ."[119] (Emphasis added.)

In Federalist Paper No. 1 - General Introduction For the Independent Journal - To the People of the State of New York, Alexander Hamilton wrote,

"AFTER an unequivocal experience of the inefficiency of the subsisting federal government, you are called upon to deliberate on a new Constitution for the United States of America. The subject speaks its own importance; comprehending in its consequences nothing less than the existence of the UNION, the safety and welfare of the parts of which it is composed, the fate of an empire in many respects the most interesting in the world. It has been frequently remarked that it seems to have been reserved to the people of this country, by their conduct and example, to decide the **important question, whether societies of men are really capable or not of establishing good government from reflection and choice, or whether they are forever destined to depend for their political constitutions on accident and force**. If there be any truth in the remark, the crisis at which we are arrived may with propriety be regarded as the era in which that decision is to be made; and a wrong election of the part we shall act may, in this view, deserve to be considered as the general misfortune of mankind. . . ."[120] (Emphasis added.)

The Constitution is considered to be the most supreme United States law in the U.S.A. The Constitution also provides power to the United States' national government to create its own money without a private central bank.

The **United States Constitution** states in Article I,

"Section. 8.

The Congress shall have Power. . . .

To borrow Money on the credit of the United States; . . . .

To coin Money, regulate the Value thereof, and of foreign Coin, and fix the Standard of Weights and Measures; . . . .

To make all Laws which shall be necessary and proper for carrying into Execution the foregoing Powers, and all other Powers vested by this Constitution in the Government of the United States, or in any Department or Officer thereof."[121] (Emphasis added.) (Also, the U.S. Constitution is in Appendix B of this book.)

I believe that the United States Supreme Court's Constitutional case law precedence very strongly supports the ability of the U.S. government to create and print its own money without a private central bank like the Federal Reserve.

The United States of America's government power to make U.S. money is considered very well-settled by Constitutional attorneys. For example, the U.S. Congressional Research Service of The Library Of Congress produced a very detailed annotated analysis and interpretation of the Constitution.

Regarding Article I, Section 8 of the Constitution, the U.S. Congressional Research Service's lengthy document states in pertinent part,

"FISCAL AND MONETARY POWERS OF CONGRESS
Coinage, Weights, and Measures
The power "to coin money" and "regulate the value thereof" <u>has been broadly construed to authorize regulation of every phase of the subject of currency</u>. Congress may charter banks and endow them with the right to issue circulating notes,1464 and it may restrain the circulation of notes not issued under its own authority.1465 To this end it may impose a prohibitive tax upon the circulation of the notes of state banks 1466 or of municipal corporations.1467 It may require the surrender of gold coin and of gold certificates in exchange for other currency not redeemable in gold. A plaintiff who sought payment for the gold coin and certificates thus surrendered in an amount measured by the higher market value of gold was denied recovery on the ground that he had not proved that he would suffer any actual loss by being compelled to accept an equivalent amount of other currency.1468 Inasmuch as "every contract for the payment of money, simply, is necessarily subject to the constitutional power of the government over the currency, whatever that power may be, and the obligation of the parties is, therefore, assumed with reference to that power," 1469 <u>the Supreme Court sustained the power of Congress to make Treasury notes **legal tender** in satisfaction of antecedent debts,1470 and, many years later, to abrogate the clauses in private</u>

<u>contracts calling for payment in gold coin, even though such contracts were executed before the legislation was passed.</u>1471 The power to coin money also imports authority to maintain such coinage as a medium of exchange at home, and to forbid its diversion to other uses by defacement, melting or exportation.1472"[122] (Emphasis added.)

Now, by the debts we have incurred through the Federal Reserve and our Federal government, I believe we are unfortunately at risk of an economic collapse if our nation continues on the same path.

However, we also have the ability to stop right now and correct this path.

The United States could and should immediately end the Federal Reserve, make our government our own central bank, reboot our economic system, and pay debts with newly issued Federal government printed money.

There might be some economic recalibration or rebooting of our currency that will cause some turbulence, but this will be much better than a collapse. This rebooting will also take time and adjustment, but the U.S. will survive and then thrive again.

If our nation's economy is destroyed, what will happen to our liberties, safety, security, private property and retirements? Obviously, this would be a terrible time.

Worse, if our nation's economy is destroyed, what will happen to the next generation? Again, this would be a terrible time.

More, if our nation's economy is destroyed, what will happen to our nation?

I believe that we cannot continue on the current path with the Federal Reserve and our enormous U.S. debt without the <u>eventual</u> destruction of our nation (or such a change to our nation that you would not even recognize it).

I hope you see the importance of protecting our nation.

Again, I disagree with Dr. Paul about his suggested solution involving <u>private</u> minters and competitive <u>private</u> central banking. The <u>one</u> central bank for the United States should <u>ONLY</u> be the United States federal government itself.

The government laws are social contracts. People agree to be held to laws. If the U.S. government passes laws through Congress that our U.S. currency has value, then it is accepted as having value when people trust the government.

What financial qualifications of the Federal Reserve are better than the qualifications of elected government officials? None.

Should people trust the Federal Reserve more than their elected government representatives? No.

Are the Federal Reserve bankers more responsive to the "Average Joe Citizen" compared to our elected government representatives? No.

Most important, is the Federal Reserve doing a good job handling the monetary system? No!

Brown strongly points out that,

"As long as the money supply is created as a debt owed back to private banks with interest, the nation's wealth will continue to be drained off into private vaults, leaving scarcity in its wake."[123]

More, Brown tells us terrible and shocking news about

96

risky derivatives and the U.S. economy,

> "The American banking system . . . has today
> become a giant betting machine. By December
> 2007, an estimated **$681 trillion** *were riding on
> complex high-risk bets known as* **derivatives** *–
> 10 times the annual output of the entire world
> economy. These* bets *are* funded by big U.S.
> banks and are made largely with borrowed
> money created on a computer screen*.
> *Derivatives can be and have been used to
> manipulate markets, look businesses, and
> destroy competitor economies."* [124] (Emphasis
> added.)

This <u>$681 Trillion</u> (Yes, with a capital "T") amount dwarfs our large U.S. debt. What happens if this derivative market crashes?

So, how much is our real U.S. economic risk? I'm not sure. But, while doing research for this book, financial rabbits keep popping out of bank magicians' hats.

Brown wrote,

> "The United States is legally bankrupt, defined in
> the dictionary as being unable to pay one's debts,
> being insolent, or having liabilities in excess of
> reasonable market value of assets held."[125]

I disagree with Brown about the U.S. being legally bankrupt. Again, the U.S. still has the power to do its own central banking, do its own credit, print its own money, and pay its own debts.

Brown adds,

> "If governments everywhere are in debt, who are
> they in debt to? The answer is that they are in

debt *to private banks*. The 'cruel hoax' is that governments are in debt for money created on a computer screen, money they could have created themselves."[126] (Emphasis added.)

The Federal Reserve website stated,

"[T]the Federal Reserve is subject to oversight by the Congress, which often reviews the Federal Reserve's activities and can alter its responsibilities by statute. Therefore, the Federal Reserve can be more accurately described as 'independent within the government' rather than 'independent of government.' . . ."[127] (Emphasis added. As indicated above, this website was changed after I already quoted part for this book, so this is no longer on the website.)

Again, this is misleading because the words "within the government" do not accurately or fully describe the relationship of the Federal Reserve and our U.S. government.

Worse, the language used by the Federal Reserve website makes is sound like the Federal government is strictly watching and controlling the Federal Reserve. This interpretation would be incorrect.

The Federal Reserve website, states in pertinent part, "The Federal Reserve is subject to oversight by Congress."[128]

Really? I don't think there was much oversight by Congress!

Congress has let the Federal Reserve be largely unmonitored, uncontrolled, and without much information to U.S. citizens.

What about an audit of the Federal Reserve?

Below is a newsworthy government article from U.S. Senator Bernie Sanders website, regarding the **first** top-to-bottom **audit** of the Federal Reserve in **2011**,

"The Fed Audit

Thursday, July 21, 2011

The *first* top-to-bottom **audit** of the Federal Reserve uncovered eye-popping new details about how the U.S. provided a whopping $16 trillion in **secret loans** to bail out American **and foreign banks and businesses** during the worst economic crisis since the Great Depression. An amendment by Sen. Bernie Sanders to the Wall Street reform law passed one year ago this week directed the Government Accountability Office to conduct the study. **'As a result of this audit, we now know** that the Federal Reserve provided *more than* **$16 trillion in total financial assistance to some of the largest financial institutions and corporations in the United States and** *throughout the world,'* said Sanders. 'This is a clear case of <u>socialism for the rich</u> and rugged, <u>you're-on-your-own individualism for everyone else</u>.'

Among the investigation's key findings is that the Fed unilaterally provided trillions of dollars in financial assistance to **foreign** banks and corporations from South Korea to Scotland, according to the GAO report. **'***No agency of the United States government* should be allowed to bailout a foreign bank or corporation without the direct approval of Congress and the president,'** Sanders said.

The non-partisan, investigative arm of Congress also determined that the Fed lacks a comprehensive system to deal with **conflicts of interest**, despite the serious potential for abuse. In fact, according to the report, the Fed provided conflict of interest waivers to employees and private contractors so they could keep investments in the same financial institutions and corporations that were given emergency loans.

For example, the CEO of JP Morgan Chase served on the New York Fed's board of directors at the same time that his bank received more than $390 billion in financial assistance from the Fed. Moreover, JP Morgan Chase served as one of the clearing banks for the Fed's emergency lending programs.

In another disturbing finding, the GAO said that on Sept. 19, 2008, William Dudley, who is now the New York Fed president, was granted a waiver to let him keep investments in AIG and General Electric at the same time AIG and GE were given bailout funds. One reason the Fed did not make Dudley sell his holdings, according to the audit, was that it might have created the appearance of a conflict of interest.

To Sanders, the conclusion is simple. 'No one who works for a firm receiving direct financial assistance from the Fed should be allowed to sit on the Fed's board of directors or be employed by the Fed,' he said.

The investigation also revealed that the Fed outsourced most of its emergency lending programs to **private contractors**, many of which also were recipients of extremely low-interest and then-secret loans.

The Fed outsourced virtually all of the operations

of their emergency lending programs to private contractors like JP Morgan Chase, Morgan Stanley, and Wells Fargo. The same firms also received trillions of dollars in Fed loans at near-zero interest rates. Altogether some two-thirds of the contracts that the Fed awarded to manage its emergency lending programs were no-bid contracts. Morgan Stanley was given the largest no bid contract worth $108.4 million to help manage the Fed bailout of AIG.

A more detailed GAO investigation into potential conflicts of interest at the Fed is due on Oct. 18, but Sanders said one thing already is abundantly clear. 'The Federal Reserve must be reformed to serve the needs of working families, not just CEOs on Wall Street.'"[129] (Emphasis added.)

Again, we know that the Federal Reserve Act was made into law in **1913**. The first top to bottom audit of the Federal Reserve was in **2011**. Let's do the math: 1913 to 2011 . . . that is almost 100 years to do a first full audit. Unbelievable! That absolutely proves the complete lack of U.S. government oversight of the Federal Reserve.

I don't agree with Senator Sanders on many things. However, I do very much like and appreciate that Senator Sanders posted the above article on his website.

The audit found numerous terrible things that needed to be discovered. I am glad that there was eventually a full audit of the Federal Reserve. The terrible things are not just that we have a huge Federal debt caused by the Federal Reserve and U.S. government. The audit also showed that the Federal Reserve had involved private, secretive, bank profiting, conflicts of interest, bailout of foreign banks, and bailout of foreign financial institutions. The audit clearly showed the unchecked nature of the Federal Reserve banking system. A huge reason that our nation is in an economic crisis is because it uses the

Federal Reserve banking system!

Yet, why hasn't anything been done about all these terrible things that the Federal Reserve has done? Most people probably don't even know about this audit.

The audit found galactic amounts of money and some outrageous things done by the Federal Reserved. Given our nation's huge debt and economic problems, why wasn't there huge television, newspaper and magazine news coverage of this audit? I'm not sure. Maybe, no one is following the money.

Here is a big part of the problem: the illusion continues even after the audit. For example, even this 2011 government article incorrectly described the Federal Reserve as a "government agency." As you know from the Federal Reserve's own recent past website (now changed), the Federal Reserve is really NOT a government agency (at least, not a government agency that is part of the Federal executive branch of our government or any branch of government). It is a private central banking system that has been authorized by Congress.

Ron Paul also points out that the government is a huge part of the problem. Paul wrote,

"The worse the economy gets, the more power Congress is willing to grant to the Federal Reserve. Who would have ever believed that it would come to this? Trillions of dollars created and distributed by the Fed with no requirement to submit to any oversight."[130]   (Emphasis added.)

In a September 27, 2016 online article by Patrick Gillespie entitled, Donald Trump claims Fed is 'more political' than Clinton, Gillespie wrote in part,

"'We have a **Fed that's doing political things** ... [ellipsis in article] the Fed is being more political than Secretary Clinton,' Trump said at Monday's presidential debate.

It's something he's been saying on the campaign trail for awhile.

Trump's central argument is that the Federal Reserve, America's central bank, is <u>keeping interest rates low to help the economy look good under Obama.</u>

Trump said earlier this month that Fed chair Janet Yellen should be 'ashamed of herself' for keeping interest rates low and <u>creating a 'false stock market.'</u>

Last week, Yellen emphatically denied any political influence."[131] (Emphasis added.)

People in different parts of politics are unhappy with the Federal Reserve. U.S. Senator Bernie Sanders is known to be more politically left. As you read earlier in my book, Senator Sanders has an article on the shocking audit of the Federal Reserve on his website. As I wrote earlier in this book, Former Congressman Dr. Ron Paul wrote that he wants to end the Federal Reserve. Donald Trump has recently become President of the United States. President Donald Trump stated many problems with the Federal Reserve. It sounds like some people might want to do some yelling at the Federal Reserve Chair Yellen!

Why hasn't the tremendous amount of money creation by the Federal Reserve worked to help our economy?

Those bankers and large corporate executives that got the <u>bailout money</u> are the winners. The money printing and lower interest rates did not help the poor because the easy money did not make jobs. The business paradigm of easy money, increasing technology, and NAFTA (open trading) caused the number of poor in the U.S. to increase.

For example, a hypothetical business would say, "Great! We got money at a very low cost. Let's beat our competitors with this free money and let's make more money!" So they invest in more technology which eventually results in needing fewer employees. More, they say, "Let's also move our manufacturing to a country that pays labor much less, has less environmental regulations, etc. Then, we will sell the products in the U.S." The result? A disastrous economy.

Some people may have received some money from unemployment insurance or from a refinanced house, but many people see no future because there are not enough family supporting jobs. The jobs are in low paying service industries. But, the top executives within banks, financial companies and corporations are extremely rich.

At the base level, our national U.S. government should REALLY and DIRECTLY be the central banking system in the U.S., not the Federal Reserve. The government should take over the Federal Reserve. Then, it will not be a secret central banking cartel. As I explained earlier in this book, I believe this should be done by a U.S. Constitutional amendment (and not just a U.S. law that can be more easily changed back) to achieve goals and prevent the yo-yo of private central banking again.

If the U.S. government would then really create money, it would cost the Federal government 0% interest. The U.S. government could then really loan money to private small banks and credit unions.

The government must be responsible so that the fiat money is trusted and valuable to the people that use it as currency. The government can't just print money, but needs to maintain a balanced annual budget and no accumulated debt.

There is another factor that we need to consider with the U.S. government taking over the U.S. central banking. The factor is the distribution of the money through private small banks.

Banks and credit unions that loan money should have anti-trust laws strongly applied so that they are not monopolies or oligopolies. (An oligopoly is similar to a monopoly, but there are some companies in an oligopoly that act together to control a large part of the market instead of just one company in a monopoly.) If the anti trust laws were enforced on banks, there would be no business considered too big to fail, and the free market system would work much more efficiently.

Without banking oligopolies or a monopoly, the consumer borrowers and business borrowers would benefit from lower loan costs. More people could buy homes and cars. Also, more businesses would be started.

The small private banks and credit unions would make money on loaning out money at a higher rate than the banks would pay to the Federal government for the money the banks receive from the Federal government. The small private banks and credit unions would also compete on banking services.

The entire government central banking system would need to be completely transparent.

Fractional reserves would not matter if deposits are issued by the same government that does its own central banking and also prints its own money. Of course, the deposits that people and businesses put in banks and credit unions could be safely insured to a point and earn interest.

Banks and credit unions could be allowed to loan an amount of money that the banks would receive directly from the Federal government central bank.

It must be easy for small private banks to be created and to exist. Then, all banks will compete more with interest rates and services.

If banks only did lending and accepted deposits, it would be a great thing for people and businesses seeking loans. Banks would concentrate on making more loans and providing other real banking services.

With more banks competing to make loans, more homes would be purchased and more business would be started. Businesses would also grow.

This competition would be a great thing for people seeking loans and for our U.S. economy.

The problems of the Federal Reserve doing our central banking are bigger than the bank bailouts, bigger than Enron, etc. The problems are also getting bigger.

When should the U.S. decide to end the Federal Reserve? Immediately.

In addition, if banks and credit unions are always prohibited from financial investments like stocks, mutual funds, derivatives and bonds, our economy will be safer.

In the next chapter, I will discuss a different problem with banking – the U.S. government's colossal mistake of repealing the Glass-Steagall Act. I will also discuss the Plunge Protection Team.

Then, in the chapter after, I will discuss the issue of our U.S. dollar as the world reserve currency, BRICS and world banking.

If you want to know where many of our nation's monetary problems come from, follow the money.

And, if you follow the money, it will lead you to the Federal Reserve.

The Federal Reserve has not helped our U.S. nation or U.S. citizens. The Federal Reserve is really doing the opposite – the Federal Reserve has caused, and is causing, huge problems for the United States of America.

I must admit, I am ***fed up*** *with the Federal Reserve!*

CHAPTER 5

GLASS-STEAGALL REPEAL MISTAKE & THE PLUNGE PROTECTION TEAM MARKET MANIPULATION

What is a bank? Picture a bank in your mind. Do you see a teller, a person making deposits at a window, and a loan desk?

Or, do you see astronomical amounts of risky investments on computer screens, etc.?

What is an investment bank? Do you have a picture of an investment bank in your mind? This is harder to picture for many people.

A definition of investment bank (IB) from Investopedia's website is,

> "[A] financial intermediary that performs a variety of services. Investment banks specialize in large and complex financial transactions such as underwriting, acting as an intermediary between a securities issuer and the investing public, facilitating mergers and other corporate reorganizations, and acting as a broker and/or financial adviser for institutional clients. . . .
>
> The advisory divisions of investment banks are paid a fee for their services, while the **trading divisions experience profit or loss** based on their market performance. Professionals who work for investment banks may have careers as financial advisers, traders or salespeople. An investment banker career can be very lucrative, but it typically comes with long hours and significant stress.

Because investment banks have external clients but *also trade their own accounts*, a **conflict of interest** can occur if the advisory and trading divisions don't maintain their independence (called the "Chinese Wall"). Investment banks' clients include corporations, pension funds, other financial institutions, governments and hedge funds. *Size is an asset for investment banks. . . .*"[132] (Emphasis added and links omitted.)

The government let the financial markets go "wild west" when it repealed the Glass-Steagall Act. This repeal caused more opportunities for banks to make more money, but it also caused much more economic instability for the banks. As you know, the instability of the banks in the USA and the world, caused instability for the U.S. economy and caused a huge U.S. debt.

In an article entitled, *Repeal of Glass-Steagall Caused the Financial Crisis, The repeal of the law separating commercial and investment banking caused the 2008 financial crisis,* James Rickards wrote in pertinent part,

"[T]he financial crisis might not have happened at all but for the **1999 repeal of the Glass-Steagall law** that **separated commercial and investment banking for seven decades**. If there is any hope of avoiding another meltdown, it's critical to understand why Glass-Steagall repeal helped to cause the crisis. Without a return to something like Glass-Steagall, another greater catastrophe is just a matter of time."[133] (Emphasis added.)

Obviously, I do not agree with Rickards on the root cause of the financial crisis. I believe that the financial crisis would have occurred even if the Glass-Steagall Act wasn't repealed. The financial crisis just might have taken much longer to develop. I do believe that the repeal of the Glass–Steagall Act was a huge mistake that was a big <u>part of</u> creating the perfect financial storm. The repeal of the Glass–Steagall Act contributed to the economic crisis.

In 2012, Barry Ritholtz wrote an article entitled, *Repeal of Glass-Steagall: Not a cause, but a multiplier.*"[134] In this article, Ritholtz argues,

> "The repeal of Glass-Steagall may not have caused the crisis — but its repeal was a factor that made it much worse. And it was a continuum of the radical deregulation movement. This philosophy incorrectly held that banks could <u>regulate themselves</u>, that government had no place in overseeing finance and that the free market works best when left alone. . . .

> As the events of 2007 to 2009 have revealed, this erroneous belief system was <u>a major factor</u> leading to the credit boom and bust, as well as the financial collapse."[135] (Emphasis added.)

I agree with Ritholtz that the repeal of the Glass-Steagall Act was deregulation that made the economic crisis worse.

Ritholtz also wrote in his article,

> "Imagine a 'but for' scenario where Glass-Steagall had not been overturned but the rest of the deregulatory actions had still taken place. Would the crisis have occurred? Without a doubt, yes.

> The Fed still would have taken rates down to unprecedented low levels. This would have led to a global spiral in asset prices. The nonbank, lend-to-sell-to-securitizer mortgage originators were still going to make subprime-mortgage loans to unqualified borrowers. Bear Stearns and

Lehman Brothers would still have overwhelmingly increased exposure to subprime mortgages. AIG would still have written trillions of dollars in credit-default swaps and other derivatives with zero reserves set against them. The largest security firms and deposit banks would still have charged headlong into the subprime securitization business. And Fannie Mae and Freddie Mac would still have belatedly chased these banks into the same subprime market . . .

Lastly, housing prices would still have run up to absurd levels and then collapsed."[136] (Emphasis added.)

I also do not agree with Ritholtz on the root reasons for the financial crisis. Some might say, the Federal Reserve's low interest rates and other tactics were unsuccessful attempts based on the wrong economic theory *to cur*e an *economy already in trouble*. I believe that the Federal Reserve's incorrect treatment of the problems made everything worse. The Federal Reserve's involvement in the economy was another factor in creating the perfect financial storm. The Federal Reserve went to the point of basically giving out free money to banks to use. The Federal Reserve *easy money* rescue tactics did not work. It just cost the United States more money and the U.S. debt rose.

In addition, the bail-outs of banks and Wall Street were attempts to stop an *economy already in crisis*. Bailouts were made at huge costs. More, I firmly believe bailouts will also not permanently work to help the macro-economy. *These attempts by the Federal Reserve and the Federal government were not the correct medicine for the macro-economic illness. The wrong medicine terribly exacerbated the illness. Bank Bailouts were the wrong thing to do.*

So, one real problem was the private Federal Reserve banking system itself. The proof of this is in the audit

113

discussed in the previous chapter. Also, it is clear that the U.S. government should be doing the U.S. central banking itself. Again, we don't need the Federal Reserve.

Another real and big problem is that the Federal Reserve and the Federal government do not see the root cause of technology changes affecting the macro-economy and the employment bubble. This root cause should have been the focus of the government many years <u>before</u> 1999. It should also still be the focus today and technology must be considered in planning for the future.

The trickle down economic theory of the Federal Reserve's easy money did not work to fix the economy.

Since people did not have jobs or were losing their jobs because of increases in technology, even the very low interest rates were unmanageable. Also, since so many people were unemployed or underemployed but were getting easy loans, the artificial bidding up of the real estate market was another secondary effect created by the Federal Reserve's misdiagnosis and treatment.

Marcus Stanley, in an article entitled, *There Are Real Reasons to Bring Back Glass-Steagall* (August 26, 2016), strongly wrote in pertinent part,

> "*There's also an understanding that the financial system was generally more stable during the 60 years in which Glass-Steagall was in force*. . . .
>
> The 2008 crisis was catastrophic for the global economy not simply because nonbank financial institutions failed, but because the problems in nonbanks spread throughout the financial system and threatened to bring down giant megabanks that <u>combined commercial and investment banking</u> . . . Glass-Steagall firewalls between Wall Street trading markets and ordinary

114

commercial banking are directly relevant to stopping this kind of <u>contagion</u>. . . .

<u>In our post-Glass-Steagall system, the largest banks emphasize trading market activities more than ever, and this shift has transformed finance</u>. . . .

[S]ince the 2008 crisis, these fundamental shifts have <u>not</u> been reversed. With the Glass-Steagall rollback, which had permitted the creation of financial conglomerates, the largest financial institutions have <u>only gotten larger since the crisis</u> and have further concentrated their hold on the banking and capital markets."[137] (Emphasis added.)

What are some examples of how the risk contagion infects more financial markets because the Glass-Steagall Act was repealed?

Stanley does an excellent job of pointing out that the repeal of the Glass-Steagall Act allowed AIG to be involved in large credit derivatives that ruined AIG.[138]

More, Stanley brilliantly points out that although Lehman Brothers was mostly an investment bank, it would not have been able to own commercial banks if the Glass-Steagall Act wasn't repealed.[139]

Stanley is right on track. We know that repeal of Glass-Steagall was wrong. We know of the economic crisis. Instead of reinstating the Glass-Steagall Act, what did Congress do? The U.S. enacted Dodd-Frank. The Dodd-Frank Act has been a failure to effectively regulate banking/financial companies.

Pam Martens and Russ Martens wrote an excellent 2014 article entitled *Dodd-Frank Versus Glass-Steagall: How Do They Compare?*[140]

In this article, Pam Martens and Russ Martens point out that Congress enacted the Glass-Steagall Act after investigating the Great Depression.[141] Pam Martens and Russ Martens explain that Congress had found that the main cause of the Great Depression was,

"Wall Street investment banks having access to savers' bank deposits to make wild speculative gambles in securities."[142]

Also, in this riveting article, Pam Martens and Russ Martens wrote about how well Glass-Steagall Act worked until it was repealed in 1999 and stated in part,

The Glass-Steagall legislation did exactly what it said it would do: it provided 'safer and more effective use of the assets of banks' by barring Wall Street investment banks from accepting deposits or being affiliated with banks accepting deposits. It prevented the "undue diversion of funds into speculative operations" by banning banks holding deposits from underwriting securities.

The 1933 Congress understood that the business of banking is to make sound loans to viable businesses to grow U.S. industry and create good jobs that underpin a sound economy. Gambling in stocks, and futures and exotic, hard to price derivatives should never be an authorized use of bank depositor funds – which are backstopped by the U.S. taxpayer."[143]

On the other hand, in this article, Pam Martens and Russ Martens contrasted how Dodd-Frank is not working well and stated in part,

"Dodd-Frank, which was addressing the exact

same type of market crash, the abuse of depositors' funds, and the biggest economic downturn since the Great Depression, did just the opposite of the Glass-Steagall Act. It allowed the abusive Wall Street banks to hold even greater amounts of insured deposits and to become ever more creative in how they abused those deposits. . . .

To a very large degree, Wall Street firms are trading stocks in their own unregulated stock exchanges called dark pools, or they're lending vast sums of money to hedge funds for wild gambles, or they're making loans to highly leveraged companies to become *more* highly-leveraged by buying out other companies – which will likely mean lots of job cuts rather than job creation along with piles of junk debt. . . .

The fate of a nation and the hopes and dreams of its children and its young, jobless graduates, hang in the balance."[144] (Emphasis added.)

Pam and Russ Martens' article make sense. Congress should act to protect our nation.

The U.S. should have learned what the Glass-Steagall did for this nation in the past and the U.S. should have never let go of it. Instead, the government repealed Glass-Steagall. Then, it made Dodd-Frank. Dodd-Frank was not Glass-Steagall. Dodd-Frank was not enough regulation to protect our nation.

Definitely, new regulations that are even stronger than the Glass-Steagall Act are needed immediately.

But, this is only a part of the solution, and this is not the full solution.

117

The U.S. government must know that current U.S. regulations are <u>not</u> working well. The U.S. should fix the problem with a new, even stronger, Glass-Steagall type of legislation again.

Instead of trying to fix the problems, many believe that the U.S. is just trying to cover-up and manipulate the market. Is this another financial illusion? You decide.

Now, let's examine the Working Group on Financial Markets (also known as, the Plunge Protection Team).

Let's look at a copy of President Ronald Reagan's Executive Order creating the Plunge Protection Team that states,

"Executive Order 12631--Working Group on Financial Markets

Source: The provisions of Executive Order 12631 of Mar. 18, 1988, appear at 53 FR 9421, 3 CFR, 1988 Comp., p. 559, unless otherwise noted.

By virtue of the authority vested in me as President by the Constitution and laws of the United States of America, and in order to establish a Working Group on Financial Markets, it is hereby ordered as follows:

Section 1. Establishment. (a) There is hereby established a Working Group on Financial Markets (Working Group). The Working Group shall be composed of:
(1) the <u>Secretary of the Treasury</u>, or his designee;
(2) the Chairman of the Board of Governors of th<u>e Federal Reserve</u> System, or his designee;

(3) the Chairman of the <u>Securities and Exchange Commission</u>, or his designee; and

(4) the Chairman of the <u>Commodity Futures Trading Commission</u>, or her designee.

(b) The Secretary of the Treasury, or his designee, shall be the <u>Chairman</u> of the Working Group.

Sec. 2. Purposes and Functions. (a) Recognizing the goals of enhancing the integrity, efficiency, orderliness, and competitiveness of our Nation's financial markets and <u>maintaining investor confidence</u>, the Working Group shall identify and consider:

(1) the major issues raised by the numerous studies on the events in the financial markets surrounding October 19, 1987, and any of those recommendations that have the potential to achieve the goals noted above; and

(2) <u>the actions</u>, <u>including governmental actions</u> under existing laws and regulations (such as policy coordination and <u>contingency planning</u>), that are appropriate to carry out these recommendations.

(b) The Working Group shall consult, as appropriate, with representatives of the various exchanges, clearinghouses, self-regulatory bodies, and with major market participants to determine private sector solutions wherever possible.

(c) The Working Group shall report to the President initially within 60 days (and periodically thereafter) on its progress and, if appropriate, its views on any recommended legislative changes.

Sec. 3. Administration. (a) The heads of Executive departments, agencies, and independent instrumentalities shall, to the extent permitted by law, provide the Working Group such

119

information as it may require for the purpose of carrying out this Order.

(b) Members of the Working Group shall serve without additional compensation for their work on the Working Group.

(c) To the extent permitted by law and subject to the availability of funds therefore, the Department of the Treasury shall provide the Working Group with such administrative and support services as may be necessary for the performance of its functions."[145] (Emphasis added.)

In an intriguing article entitled *Juicing the Stock Market[,] The secret maneuverings of the Plunge Protection Team*, Mike Whitney wrote in pertinent part,

"US manufacturing is <u>already in recession</u>, the dollar continues to weaken, consumer spending is flat, and the sub-prime market in real estate has begun to nosedive. These have all contributed to the markets' erratic behavior and created the likelihood that the Plunge Protection Team may be <u>stealthily</u> intervening <u>behind the scenes</u>.

According to John Crudele of the New York Post, the Plunge Protection Team's (PPT) modus operandi was revealed by a former member of the Federal Reserve Board, Robert Heller. Heller said that disasters could be mitigated by 'buying market averages in the futures market, thus <u>stabilizing the market as a whole</u>.' This appears to be the strategy that has been used.

Former-Clinton advisor, George Stephanopoulos, verified the existence of The Plunge Protection Team (as well as its methods) in an appearance on Good Morning America on Sept 17, 2000. Stephanopoulos said:

120

'[V]arious efforts that are going on in public and behind the scenes by the Fed and other government officials to **guard against a free-fall in the markets**.... [ellipsis in article] perhaps the most important the Fed in 1989 created what is called the Plunge Protection Team, which is the Federal Reserve, big major banks, representatives of the New York Stock Exchange and the other exchanges and they have been meeting informally so far, and they have a kind of an informal agreement among major banks to come in and start to buy stock if there appears to be a problem. They have in the past acted more formally... [ellipsis in article]
[Note: I added additional ellipsis here] . . . .
And they, with the guidance of the Fed, all of the banks got together when it started to collapse and **propped up** the currency markets. And, they have plans in place to consider that if the markets start to fall.'

Stephanopoulos' comments have <u>never been</u> officially denied. . . ."[146] (Emphasis added.)

As may be seen on the Internet, others have also written on the Plunge Protection Team. There appears to be some real secrecy on the Plunge Protection Team.

For example, in an online article (February 11, 2010) entitled, *Plot thickens in the battle of "The Plunge"*, John Crudele wrote,

"The PWG [i.e., President's Working Group on Financial Markets or Plunge Protection Team] operates in <u>total secrecy</u>. Members include the heads of the Treasury, the Federal Reserve and financial exchanges, but there is no record of who else participates. . . ."[147]

Crudele's article also indicated that he did a Freedom of Information Act (FOIA) request, and he received only 177 pages (but, 53 of the 177 pages had something redacted).[148] On appeal of his FOIA request, he learned that there were an additional 739 pages of PWG documents that the Treasury withheld in full.[149]

A Feb 23, 2015 article by "Tyler Durden" entitled, *Ex-Plunge Protection Team Whistleblower: 'Governments Control Markets; There Is No Price Discovery Anymore'* describes the Plunge Protection Team (also known as the Working Group on Financial Markets created by U.S. President Ronald Reagan's Executive Order one year after the crash of the stock market in 1987).[150]

In this article, "Durden" also wrote,

"Conspiracy theorists believe, however, that the real task of this committee is to <u>protect against a renewed slump in the stock market</u>. . . .

[A]s Dr. Pippa Malmgren - a former member of the U.S. President's Working Group on Financial Markets - it is not conspiracy theory, it is conspiracy fact: 'there's no price discovery anymore by the market... [ellipsis in article] governments impose prices on the market.'"[151] (Emphasis added.)

Is the Plunge Protection Team real? I don't know for sure. It is possible. I pointed out some strong statements about it. But, if it is true, it is a secret. Also, if it is true, it must involve some extremely large amounts of money.

How could the Plunge Protection Team manipulate the stock markets and/or other markets? The Plunge Protection Team has some extremely powerful financial people and entities, including the U.S. Treasury, the Federal Reserve, the

Securities and Exchange Commission, and the Commodity Futures Trading Commission.

If the Plunge Protection Team is really manipulating the financial markets, why would that be bad? It would be like a drug. It would not be real.

The problem with manipulations of the financial markets is that the markets would not be real "free markets." The financial markets would be controlled and "fixed." If the markets are fixed, no one that is not part of the manipulation would be able to correctly value financial markets. Therefore, the markets would not be fair to those that are not insiders. Also, manipulations of the financial markets could only be a temporary safety net. A continuously fixed financial market would probably eventually collapse.

In addition, if the financial markets are manipulated, do big investors and everyday people really and immediately take on their full investment risks? I believe the answer would be, "No."

If there is no price adjustment according to the true value of the financial markets, the markets are just a house of cards waiting to fall from the smallest wind. On the other hand, it is also concerning that the Plunge Protection Team could fail and our economy would not be ready for that bust.

An artificial bubble is caused by manipulations of financial markets. This type of bubble is just pushed forward and growing. The problems are not being solved and would eventually pop.

Manipulations of the financial markets are not the same as freezing or suspending financial markets. As you know, I believe manipulating financial markets would be the wrong thing to do.

On the other hand, if done in appropriate situations and

with the proper authority, freezing markets might allow people to calm down and rationalize their decisions. Freezing financial markets might also give appropriate government authorities some time to fix system problems or to handle emergencies.

Think of all the time and effort that would be involved with constantly monitoring and manipulating financial markets. The time and efforts would be better placed on fixing the market problems instead of trying to manipulate the markets. The time and money would also be much better spent on building a great and fair economy.

In the next chapter, we will look at some international banking developments in the world.

CHAPTER 6

IMF, WORLD BANK AND BRICS

Ellen Hodgson Brown wrote,

"Today, Federal Reserve Notes and U.S. dollar loans <u>dominate the economy of the world</u>; but this international currency is not money issued by the American people or their government. It is money created and lent by a private cartel of international bankers, and this <u>cartel has the United States itself hopelessly entangled in a web of debt</u>."[152] (Emphasis added.)

Why is our U.S. money so valuable to governments throughout the world?

Why do people in other countries value the U.S. dollar?

Some might say that the <u>only</u> reason that our U.S. dollar is highly valued is because the U.S. dollar has come to be widely known as the "petrodollar." I would disagree. Our nation's freedom is the <u>main</u> reason that our U.S. money is so valuable. But, the status of U.S. money as the petrodollar has been a factor.

What is the petrodollar?

A helpful online definition of the petrodollars apparently from Georgetown University (http://faculty.georgetown.edu/imo3/petrod/define.htm) states in pertinent part,

"Petrodollars may be <u>defined</u> as the U.S. dollar earned from the sale of oil, or they may be simply

126

defined as oil revenues denominated in U.S. dollars. . . .

Since petrodollars and petrodollar surpluses are by definition denominated in U.S. dollars, then purchasing power is dependent on the U.S. rate of inflation and the rate at which the U.S. dollar is exchanged (whenever there is need for convertibility) by other currencies in international money markets. **It follows that whenever economic or other factors affect the U.S. dollar, petrodollars will be affected to the same magnitude. The link, therefore, between the U.S. dollar and petrodollar surpluses, in particular, has significant economic, political, and other implications.**"[153] (Emphasis added.)

There are many currencies in the world. Why does the U.S. Money have the status of the petrodollar?

On the Follow the Money (ftmdaily.com) website, Jerry Robinson wrote the following about the petrodollar,

"**In the final days of World War II**, 44 leaders from all of the Allied nations met in **Bretton Woods**, New Hampshire in an effort to create a new global economic order. With much of the global economy decimated by the war, the United States emerged as the world's new economic leader. . . .

In addition to introducing a number of global financial agencies, the historic meeting also created an international gold-backed monetary standard which relied heavily upon the U.S. Dollar.

Initially, this dollar system worked well. However, by the 1960's, the weight of the system upon the

United States became unbearable. On **August 15, 1971**, President Richard M. Nixon shocked the global economy when he officially ended the international convertibility from U.S. dollars into gold, thereby bringing an official end to the Bretton Woods arrangement.

Two years later, . . . another system was created called the **petrodollar** system. In **1973**, a deal was struck between Saudi Arabia and the United States in which every barrel of oil purchased from the Saudis would be denominated in U.S. dollars. . . .

By **1975**, all of the OPEC nations had agreed to price their own oil supplies exclusively in U.S. dollars in exchange for weapons and military protection.

This petrodollar system, or more simply known as an 'oil for dollars' system, created an immediate artificial demand for U.S. dollars around the globe."[154] (Emphasis added. Reformatted.)

Think of the analysis of technology and the economy again for a minute. As technology advances, we will probably not need fossil fuels like petroleum (e.g., gasoline).

Eventually, any money based on petroleum, including the petrodollar, will likely be a thing of the past.

Think of the economic changes that could occur if almost all cars ran on electricity.

What is the International Monetary Fund (IMF)? What role does the IMF organization? According to the IMF Website, the IMF was created in Bretton Woods, New Hampshire, U.S.A., in 1944.[155] (Emphasis added.)

The IMF's website states in pertinent part that,

"The International Monetary Fund (IMF) is an
organization of 189 countries, working to foster
global monetary cooperation, secure financial
stability, facilitate international trade, promote high
employment and sustainable economic growth,
and reduce poverty around the world."[156]

The IMF website has a portion entitled "History" that
states in part,

"Globalization and the Crisis (2005 - present)

The implications of the continued rise of capital
flows for economic policy and the stability of the
international financial system are still not entirely
clear. The current credit crisis and the food and
oil price shock are clear signs that new
challenges for the IMF are waiting just around the
corner."[157] (Emphasis added.)

No doubt, the IMF has been, and still is, a very important
and powerful world financial institution. The IMF is located in
Washington, D.C., U.S.A.[158]

What is the World Bank? The World Bank's website
describes that it was created in 1944.[159]

The World Bank's headquarters is also in Washington,
D.C., U.S.A.[160] The World Bank's website also states in part,

"Reconstruction remains an important part of our
work. However, at today's World Bank, poverty
reduction through an inclusive and sustainable
globalization remains the overarching goal of our
work. . . ."[161]

No doubt, the World Bank also has been, and still

is, a very important and powerful world financial institution.

But, some countries are already beginning to make moves partially away from the IMF, the World Bank, and the U.S. dollar as the standard.

Other countries in the world are starting to use alternative currencies instead of the U.S. petrodollar.

In the 2014 article *'Colder War' And The End Of The Petrodollar*, Marin Katusa, wrote,

> "The mainstream media are falling over themselves talking about Russia's just-signed … gas deal with China, which is expected to be worth more than $400 billion. . . .
>
> China's President Xi Jinping has publicly stated that it's time for a new model of security, not just for China, but for all of Asia. This new model of security, otherwise known as "the new UN," will include Russia and Iran, but not the United States or the EU-28. . . .
>
> *You can bet the Russians won't take payment in U.S. dollars for their gas. This is the beginning of the end for the petrodollar. . . .*
>
> *The Chinese and Russians are working together against the Americans, and there are many countries that would be happy to join them in dethroning the U.S. dollar as the world's reserve currency. This historic gas deal between Russia and China is very bad news for the* **petrodollar**. . . .
>
> We are now in the early stages of the Colder War."[162] (Emphasis added.)

From this relevant article, you see how changes are occurring, and conflicts are growing, between different economies in the world.

What are Brazil, Russia, India, China and South Africa (BRICS) doing about the U.S. petrodollar?

In a July 16, 2014 excellent article entitled *BRICS Nations To Form Bank To Rival World Bank, IMF*, Silvio Izquierdo wrote,

> The first president of the New Development Bank will be from India and the position will rotate every five years among **Brazil, Russia, India, China and South Africa — the so-called *BRICS* nations**, a joint statement from the leaders said.
>
> BRICS leaders conferred in a closed session earlier in the day at their conference in northeastern Brazil, then announced concrete plans for the bank at an afternoon session open to the press.
>
> ***The new bank is seen as a strong push by the BRICS <u>against the World Bank and the International Monetary Fund</u>, which the developing world has <u>long complained it (sic) far too U.S.- and European-centric</u>.***"[163]
> (Emphasis added.)

In a July 28, 2014 article entitled, *The BRICS Bank Is Born Out of Politics*, John Hartley wrote,

> "This past week marked the 70th anniversary of the Bretton Woods agreement, which reshaped the international financial system by creating both the International Monetary Fund and the World Bank. Fortuitously, this month also marks the

creation of the new so-called 'BRICS Bank' . . ."[164]

This BRICS Bank is a <u>large change in world banking</u>. This is a very strange and unusual time in the world.

Hartley also wrote in this article,

"There is also an outstanding question of whether the *BRICS Bank formation resembles a **defection from the U.S.-domiciled IMF**. . . . **The BRICS Bank, along with the proposed BRICS Fuel Reserve Bank, would <u>not</u> be required to keep their assets in U.S. dollars**."[165] (Emphasis added.)

I believe that the BRICS Bank did not coincidentally come to fruition at the same time that the United States is attempting to recover from an economic crisis. Logically, the <u>stability, strength and integrity</u> of the U.S. dollar are also likely precipitating reasons for the BRICS Bank formation. Because some U.S. banks recently needed bailing out, the U.S. dollar probably doesn't look so good to the rest of the world. Therefore, the financial crisis in the U.S. is probably a major factor in the formation of BRICS.

However, politics are obviously another likely reason that some foreign countries wanted to form the BRICS Bank. The integrity, stability and strength of a country does matter in politics. In IMF politics, the country's GDP (production) strength is a factor in voting power.

Of course, international finances and politics are interwoven. Often, the issues and influences of international finances and politics are difficult to even distinguish. Furthermore, international finances and politics are not always mutually exclusive reasons for changes in world banking.

When I phonetically hear "BRICS," I think of a brick wall.

If we have goodwill and good relations in the world, it would be less likely that anyone would want to build a brick bank wall without including the United States.

Some new developments occurred in the IMF recently. A page from the IMF's website dated Sept. 30, 2016 with a title "*Special Drawing Right SDR*" states,

> "The SDR is an international reserve asset, created by the IMF in 1969 to supplement its member countries' official reserves. As of March 2016, 204.1 billion SDRs (equivalent to about $285 billion) had been created and allocated to members. SDRs can be exchanged for freely usable currencies. The value of the SDR is based on a basket of five major currencies—the U.S. dollar, euro, the Chinese renminbi (RMB) [i.e., the yuan], the Japanese yen, and pound sterling—as of October 1, 2016.

The role of the SDR

The SDR was created by the IMF in 1969 as a supplementary international reserve asset, in the context of the Bretton Woods fixed exchange rate system. A country participating in this system needed official reserves—government or central bank holdings of gold and widely accepted foreign currencies—that could be used to purchase its domestic currency in foreign exchange markets, as required to maintain its exchange rate. But the international supply of two key reserve assets— gold and the U.S. dollar—proved inadequate for supporting the expansion of world trade and financial flows that was taking place. Therefore, the international community decided to create a new international reserve asset under the auspices of the IMF.

Only a few years after the creation of the SDR, the Bretton Woods system collapsed and the major currencies shifted to floating exchange rate regimes. Subsequently, the growth in international capital markets facilitated borrowing by creditworthy governments and many countries accumulated significant amounts of international reserves. These developments lessened the reliance on the SDR as a global reserve asset. However, more recently, the 2009 SDR allocations totaling SDR 182.6 billion played a critical role in providing liquidity to the global economic system and supplementing member countries' official reserves amid the global financial crisis. . . ."[166] (Emphasis added.)

A Sept. 29, 2016 Bloomberg News online article entitled *Chinese Yuan's Ascent to Global Reserve Status: A Timeline* stated,

"The yuan will become one of five global reserve currencies on Saturday [Oct. 1, 2016], the culmination of several years of efforts by Chinese policy makers to gain such recognition.

Its entry into the International Monetary Fund's Special Drawing Rights -- alongside the dollar, euro, pound and the yen -- *will help further China's efforts to boost international usage of the yuan*. . . ."[167] (Emphasis added.)

(As I have been writing this book, there continues to be large and rapid changes in the world and U.S. economy. Of course, I might never finish this book if I continued to try to research and write about changes.)

In the past, being a U.S. citizen was important for financial reasons. This is true still today.

In the past, many people in the world also wanted to be U.S. citizens because of the freedoms and rights we have in the U.S.A. This is also still true today.

U.S. citizens still enjoy the most freedom of any large country in the world.

More, other countries in the world wanted to be like the United States of America. The values and integrity that the U.S. exemplified were large reasons for the United States of America's leadership role in the world. The United States' Republic form of government was also admired because of our checks and balances on the branches of our government. The United States of America was respected.

Our U.S. Constitutional rights have been the main value of country. What value do you put on freedom? Many people have died fighting for these Constitutional rights. We need to protect our valuable Constitutional rights.

I am concerned that the U.S. government's, and the other nations', failure to see that technology changes are affecting the world's macro-economy might eventually result in a devastating financial crisis in many parts of the world. In addition, I am concerned that the Federal Reserve banking system, the astronomical U.S. debt, and the repeal of the Glass-Steagall regulations will lead to serious U.S. and world financial crisis. I am also concerned that financial and/or other conflicts might arise.

Of course, the U.S. should fully attempt to always avoid a major financial crisis and, especially, other types of conflicts such as war.

I need not elaborate further about the reasons we should always fully attempt to always avoid financial conflicts and wars.

I see the real conflict as a battle for people's hearts. I

will elaborate on this more later.

The United States should do its best to be the world leader in production. We have the ability to use technology, people and natural resources. We need a plan on how to deal with our technology, workers and macro-economy. We need to respect and obey our U.S. Constitution.

The U.S. also should do our best to use our leadership and technology like a good neighbor to other developing nations. Good relationships with other countries don't just help other countries. Good relationships with other countries also help the U.S. When the U.S. shows that it cares for our world neighbors, things run more smoothly for the U.S. and the world. There is a synergy when countries truly work together cooperatively.

Ron Paul wrote about some problems that would occur with a world currency and important reasons why we should not want a world currency. Paul wrote,

> "As a way to patch up the system, there is now new talk of the old Keynesian dream of a world currency. I seriously doubt that it will happen. It will falter for the same reason that it has always faltered: nationalist pressure. It is one thing to create a new composite currency for Europe. Not even that is entirely stable. But the world elites will not likely get their act together in a way that would do the same for the world.
>
> I'm happy about that. It is true that a world currency would achieve great gains in terms of efficiency. The classical gold standard was a world currency of sorts, albeit with different names for national currencies. This is an ideal I would like to see restored. But a world currency of fiat paper money would be even more vulnerable to inflationary pressure than the

current system. <u>The last check on inflationary finance that remains in the system is the prospect of a falling value of one currency relative to others. A new world currency would remove that one check, however ineffective it is</u>."[168] (Emphasis added.)

Again, I disagree with Ron Paul on the gold standard move now. I also think that the efficiency of a world gold standard would quickly diminish because:

- a world currency would be a precursor to a world government;
- a world government would quickly become totalitarian without freedoms; and
- a totalitarian government and serfdom/slavery is never efficient (and never acceptable).

A world currency would be without a check of a comparison of one currency to other currencies. This is a mistake that would leave the central bank of the world without competition.

A world currency would be a huge mistake. When people talk about a world currency, tell them to remember the U.S. Revolution and other history. We need to protect the independence and sovereignty of the United States of America.

More, Ellen Hodgson Brown's book includes that Dr. Carrol Quigley wrote,

"[F]rom personal knowledge that an elite clique of global financiers are bent on controlling the world. Their aim, [Quigley] said, was 'nothing less than to create a <u>world system of financial control</u> in <u>private</u> hands able to <u>dominate </u>the political system of each country and the economy of the <u>world as a whole</u>.'"[169] (Emphasis added.)

I don't know who these financiers are, or if this is true

137

now. But, the current private Federal Reserve fiat money central banking system is siphoning the wealth from our nation. Also, as indicated in other parts of this book, foreigners were part of previous central banks in the U.S. More, as the audit of the Federal Reserve uncovered, the Federal Reserve has provided money to foreign banks and corporations. Recently, I have heard repeated political discussions that include the idea of a "new world order" or "one world government." That makes me wonder if the quote of Dr. Carrol Quigley could be true!

I do not want a one world government. Where could you go if a "one world government" was created and it became tyrannical? You couldn't go anywhere to escape the tyranny.

Likewise, many of us take for granted our Constitutional rights, but people in other nations do not enjoy these freedoms. A "one world government" may not even start with these precious rights.

Would ruthless, powerful, and wealthy people do ruthless, power-grabbing, wealth-taking things if they could? From history, I would say, "Yes."

We have a Republic form of government and a U.S. Constitution to guard against government abuses and to protect our citizens.

Think about this: Would a one world government allow:

Religious freedom;

Freedom of speech;

Freedom of the press;

Right to a jury trial;

Right to bear arms;

Right to own property; and

Other rights?

Again, I remind everyone: people in other countries do not have rights like we do in the U.S.A.

We also have the checks and balances of power in the U.S.A. We know the checks and balances of Congress against the President, of the President against the Supreme Court, of the Supreme Court against Congress, etc. These checks and balances should act like a homeostasis of our national government so that no one branch ever gets too much power over the citizens.

The fact that there are other governments in the world provides competition between nations. People leave bad nations. When people leave bad nations, they take their wealth and education with them.

More, even if there were constitutional rights and even if there were checks and balances in a one world government, over time these would likely erode. Also, the larger the government, the easier it is for the government to eventually take away the individual rights of the citizens.

Again, we need to keep the Constitution, sovereignty, and independence of the U.S.A.

In the next chapter, we will discuss what could happen if the economic crisis is not correctly addressed.

CHAPTER 7

WHAT IF THE ECONOMIC CRISIS IS <u>NOT</u> CORRECTLY ADDRESSED?

What if the economic crisis is not correctly addressed?

If fully researched, well-reasoned, fully debated, and public analysis of the economic challenges caused by the transition from the Industrial Age to the Information Age are not made, economic planning will be like traveling without a guide, map, compass, or (even without) a chosen destination.

More, if we don't look at the effect that changes in technology have on economics, we won't be able to make strategic plans for the benefit of our citizens, our nation, and friends throughout the world.

The U.S. macro-economy has never been impacted by technology as quickly and as powerfully as is seen in this Information Age. The Information Age is still in its early childhood stage of development. The number of changes caused by the new Information Age could be almost countless. In addition, the new, fast and large effects of technology on the economy, makes this analysis very difficult.

Our U.S. government and the Federal Reserve bankers won't be able to keep up the illusion forever. The printing of fiat money by a private central bank that is not fully controlled by the citizens with government checks and balances (and with complete transparency) is sure to be for the benefit of the oligarchies, wealthy individuals and the politically connected cronies.

If we don't take control of our U.S. economy by creating our own central bank run by the government, we won't be able to steer our economy for the financial prosperity of our U.S.

citizens and our sovereign U.S. nation.

If we don't take control of our U.S. debt, U.S. fiscal plans, and U.S. government's policies, our nation will continue to be in trouble and our citizens will eventually suffer much more.

Many books have been written about a dystopian future society ruined by the wrong uses of technology, unopposed greed, and consolidation of government power. More, many of these fictional stories involve the stripping away of citizens' inalienable rights and some form of serfdom. Are we really headed more in that direction? Possibly.

Predictions are hard to make with any accuracy.

We should not let fear control us into a self-fulfilling negative prophesy. We must keep positive attitudes and make positive changes. Still, I will try to make some predictions on what is possibly ahead on our current path. But remember, we can still change our path.

HERE ARE MY <u>KAFKAS' TOP 25 PREDICTIONS</u> OF THINGS THAT WILL HAPPEN *IF* THE ECONOMIC CRISIS IS NOT CORRECTLY ADDRESSED:

1. Technology will continue to increase in computers, robotics, manufacturing, science, medicine, pharmaceutical, physics, military, communications, entertainment and many other areas. Technology will continue to permeate almost all aspects of our society.
2. The world population of potential workers (labor supply) will continue to increase.
3. The need for human workers (labor demand) will decrease. Unemployment rate will continue to increase.
4. Demand for many discretionary consumer products will decrease.
5. Home foreclosures will increase.
6. Children and families will needlessly suffer. There will

be increased stress on families, children, and relationships. There will be an increased number of divorces.

7. Without jobs, people won't be able to pay their bills. There will be an increased number of bankruptcies.
8. The sector of the population dependent on various government benefits will increase.
9. The government benefits will also become meager.
10. Unemployed people and their families that are living in high unemployment urban areas will be like people living in new government "serfdoms." The government will take more control of their lives. The people will give up more of their individual rights. People will go from being web "surfers" to living in "serfdoms."
11. The amount of production (and then only potential production) will continue to increase (for example, factories can run 24 hours/day/7 days a week with robotics).
12. Production costs will continue to decrease.
13. Retail and wholesale costs for most items will generally decrease.
14. Information will continue to become more accessible because of computers, the Internet and other technology.
15. Some large companies in certain markets will continue to show large profits, growth, etc.
16. A small number of people will become super wealthy.
17. Alternative energy systems will be brought out for marketing to the public that are already invented or that will be invented. For example, these other technologies will continue to replace fossil/petroleum based fuels.
18. More U.S. citizens and foreigners will lose trust in the U.S. government and in the Federal Reserve. Other currencies will continue to replace the U.S. petrodollar in international transactions.
19. The U.S. debt will continue to grow to astronomical amounts.
20. Our U.S. dollar will be very much devalued. Almost everything will cost a lot of money to buy.

21. Economic recessions/depressions will become bigger, will become more long-term, and will repeat (or never end for many decades). There will be an economic collapse that will affect most of the world.
22. Without proper forethought, the additional U.S. government modifications will likely be misguided, extreme, counter-productive to free market efficiencies, contrary to democracy, and violate our U.S. Constitution. This could involve marital law.
23. There will be increased talk of world depopulation and population control.
24. There will be increased financial conflicts, legal disputes, and military wars in the world. (But, I pray that there will be peace).
25. People will demand changes in governments.

Remember, you need to firmly understand that these are just my subjective views of the possible future. These are definitely <u>not</u> sure things. More, remember, these are things I predict possible **_if_** (and this is literally a big "if") the economic crisis is not correctly addressed. Corrections to our economy and government could prevent many of my predictions.

Getting too excited could be counter-productive. For example, in football, huge guys are trying to tackle the quarterback all the time, but the quarterback has to keep focused. So, as the famous football quarterback, Aaron Rogers, said, "Relax."

If we want to change things, we can still change things now.

In the final chapter of this book, I offer some possible solutions.

CHAPTER 8

SOLUTIONS TO THE ECONOMIC CRISIS

Before we look at my suggested solutions, we need to want to change things. If we don't want to change things, things won't change.

Did you ever wake someone up from a dream and the person you woke up said, "I wish you didn't wake me up because I was having the best dream."

Many people are still asleep and dreaming while our nation is in economic crisis.

Would anyone want someone to wake them if their house was on fire? Absolutely, yes!

However, some people just don't want someone to wake them to the truth about our economic crisis. They just prefer not to deal with it and to keep dreaming. So, they will probably not deal with our economic crisis until some big change happens or until there is an economic collapse.

As a nation, we need to understand the realities of our economic crisis before we deal with it.

We need to try to wake people up from the dream so that solutions can be reasonably discussed, debated and agreed upon. But, we can't force them to be awake.

Since we are a government of the people, we need to participate in our government.

Since we are the government, we can control and change our government.

In order to have change, we need to understand and admit that our nation is in a crisis and that we need to make changes to our U.S. Constitution and laws. We can't bury our heads in the sand and say we don't know about our nation's problems. Again, since we are a government by the people, we have a duty to learn about and to participate in, our government.

So, what are my suggested solutions?

In my opinion, we need to actually make Amendments to our United States Constitution and make new U.S. laws.

We all think a king can be a tyrant. In addition, a democracy, mob, president and Congress can also be tyrannical. Now, the best chance at avoiding tyranny is our Constitutional Republic with a caveat. The caveat is that the Constitution, the Rule of Law, the checks and balances of the branches of Federal government, the checks and balances of the states versus the national governments, <u>must be known and used by our citizens</u>.

As I wrote earlier in this book, our government is made up of many treasures.

In the U.S.A., we have many treasures, but we don't know about all of them.

If you have a treasure, and you don't know that you have a treasure, it does you no good. More, if you have a treasure and you don't know it, it might be taken from you. This is true even if someone has a treasure in their own house. We have treasures in our own house – that is in our own U.S. government, but we don't fully know it.

More, if we don't know where the treasures are located, it is almost impossible to find them. It is like having a treasure chest buried somewhere in the U.S.A. without a map. You could be standing right on it, or go right passed it, but it doesn't make you wealthy.

Our Founding Fathers did many great things and acted courageously to create our nation. Our Founding Fathers gave us treasures (i.e., freedoms) and a treasure map (i.e., Constitution).

At the same time, we know our nation's Founding Fathers were just men and had flaws. For example, Benjamin Franklin wrote a book about his efforts to examine his own faults and his intent to be a better person.[170] Franklin wrote,

> "I ENTER'D (sic) UPON THE EXECUTION of this plan for self-examination, and continu'd (sic) it with occasional intermissions for some time. _I was surpris'd (sic) to find myself so much fuller of faults than I had imagined_; but I had the satisfaction of seeing them diminish."[171]

All of our Founding Fathers were smart enough to know that they were not perfect. In the same way, they must have also known that they could not make a perfect Constitution. Therefore, our Founding Fathers wisely included in our U.S. Constitution several ways to peacefully amend the Constitution.

More, President George Washington even forecasted a need for amendments to the Constitution. (As you will read, President Washington also wrote of our nation's independence, the preservation of liberty, the checks and balances of powers, his warnings of Federal debt, his warnings of foreign influence, etc.)

Below are some pertinent and helpful parts of a transcript of President George Washington's beautiful and patriotic **Farewell Address** (1796):

"Friends and Fellow Citizens:

. . . .

150

Here, perhaps, I ought to stop. But a solicitude for your welfare, which cannot end but with my life, and the apprehension of danger, natural to that solicitude, urge me, on an occasion like the present, to offer to your solemn contemplation, and to recommend to your frequent review, some sentiments which are the result of much reflection, of no inconsiderable observation, and which appear to me all-important to the permanency of your felicity as a people. <u>These will be offered to you with the more freedom, **as you can only see in them the disinterested warnings of a parting friend, who can possibly have no personal motive to bias his counsel**</u>. . . .

For this you have every inducement of sympathy and interest. Citizens, by birth or choice, of a common country, that country has a right to concentrate your affections. <u>The name of</u> **American**, which belongs to you in your national capacity, must always exalt the just pride of patriotism more than any appellation derived from local discriminations. With slight shades of difference, you have the same religion, manners, habits, and political principles. You have in a common cause fought and triumphed together; the <u>independence</u> and <u>liberty</u> you possess are the work of joint counsels, and joint efforts of common dangers, sufferings, and successes. . . . Here every portion of our country finds the most commanding motives for carefully guarding and preserving the union of the whole. . . .

To the efficacy and permanency of your Union, a government for the whole is indispensable. No alliance, however strict, between the parts can be an adequate substitute; they must inevitably experience the infractions and interruptions which

151

all alliances in all times have experienced. Sensible of this momentous truth, you have improved upon your first essay, by the adoption of a **constitution** of government better calculated than your former for an intimate union, and for the efficacious management of your common concerns. This government, the offspring of our own choice, uninfluenced and unawed, adopted upon full investigation and mature deliberation, completely free in its principles, in the distribution of its powers, uniting security with energy, and ***containing within itself a provision for its own amendment***, has a just claim to your confidence and your support. Respect for its authority, compliance with its laws, acquiescence in its measures, are duties enjoined by the fundamental maxims of true liberty. **The basis of our political systems is the right of the people to make *and to alter their constitutions of government*.** . . .

It is important, likewise, that the habits of thinking in a free country should inspire caution in those entrusted with its administration, to confine themselves within their respective constitutional spheres, avoiding in the exercise of the powers of one department to encroach upon another. The spirit of encroachment tends to consolidate the powers of all the departments in one, and thus to create, whatever the form of government, a real despotism. A just estimate of that love of power, and proneness to abuse it, which predominates in the human heart, is sufficient to satisfy us of the truth of this position. The necessity of reciprocal checks in the exercise of political power, by dividing and distributing it into different depositaries, and constituting each the guardian of the public weal against invasions by the others, has been evinced by experiments ancient and modern; some of them in our country and under

152

our own eyes. To preserve them must be as necessary as to institute them. **If, in the opinion of the people, the distribution or modification of the constitutional powers be in any particular wrong, let it be corrected by an amendment in the way which the Constitution designates.** But let there be no change by usurpation; for though this, in one instance, may be the instrument of good, it is the customary weapon by which free governments are destroyed. The precedent must always greatly overbalance in permanent evil any partial or transient benefit, which the use can at any time yield.

Of all the dispositions and habits which lead to political prosperity, religion and morality are indispensable supports. In vain would that man claim the tribute of patriotism, who should labor to subvert these great pillars of human happiness, these firmest props of the duties of men and citizens. The mere politician, equally with the pious man, ought to respect and to cherish them. A volume could not trace all their connections with private and public felicity. Let it simply be asked: Where is the security for property, for reputation, for life, if the sense of religious obligation desert the oaths which are the instruments of investigation in courts of justice? And let us with caution indulge the supposition that morality can be maintained without religion. Whatever may be conceded to the influence of refined education on minds of peculiar structure, reason and experience both forbid us to expect that national morality can prevail in exclusion of religious principle.

It is substantially true that virtue or morality is a necessary spring of popular government. The rule, indeed, extends with more or less force to every species of free government. Who that is a sincere friend to it can look with indifference upon attempts to shake the foundation of the fabric?

Promote then, as an object of primary importance, <u>institutions for the general diffusion of knowledge</u>. In proportion as the structure of a government gives force to public opinion, <u>it is essential that public opinion should be enlightened</u>.

As a very important source of strength and security, cherish <u>public credit</u>. One method of preserving it is to use it as sparingly as possible, avoiding occasions of expense by cultivating peace, but remembering also that timely disbursements to prepare for danger frequently prevent much greater disbursements to repel it, **avoiding likewise the accumulation of debt,** not only by shunning occasions of expense, but by vigorous exertion in time of peace to discharge the debts which unavoidable wars may have occasioned, not ungenerously throwing upon posterity the burden which we ourselves ought to bear. The execution of these maxims belongs to your representatives, but it is necessary that public opinion should co-operate. To facilitate to them the performance of their duty, it is essential that you should practically bear in mind that towards the payment of debts there must be revenue; that to have revenue there must be taxes; that no taxes can be devised which are not more or less inconvenient and unpleasant; that the intrinsic embarrassment, inseparable from the selection of the proper objects (which is always a choice of difficulties), ought to be a decisive motive for a candid construction of the conduct of the government in making it, and for a spirit of acquiescence in the measures for obtaining revenue, which the public exigencies may at any time dictate. . . . Against the insidious wiles of foreign influence (I conjure you to believe me, fellow-citizens) the jealousy of a free people ought to **be constantly <u>awake</u>**, since history and experience prove that <u>foreign influence is one of the most baneful foes of republican government.</u> . . .

It is our true policy to steer clear of permanent alliances with any portion of the foreign world; so far, I mean, as we are now at liberty to do it; for let me not be understood as capable of patronizing infidelity to existing engagements. I hold the maxim no less applicable to public than to private affairs, <u>that honesty is always the best policy.</u> I repeat it, therefore, let those engagements be observed in their genuine sense. But, in my opinion, it is unnecessary and would be unwise to extend them.

Taking care always to keep ourselves by suitable establishments on a respectable defensive posture, we may safely trust to temporary alliances for extraordinary emergencies.

Harmony, liberal intercourse with all nations, are recommended by policy, humanity, and interest. But even our commercial policy should hold an equal and impartial hand; neither seeking nor granting exclusive favors or preferences; consulting the natural course of things; diffusing and diversifying by gentle means the streams of commerce, but forcing nothing; establishing (with powers so disposed, in order to give trade a stable course, to define the rights of our merchants, and to enable the government to support them) conventional rules of intercourse, the best that present circumstances and mutual opinion will permit, but temporary, and liable to be from time to time abandoned or varied, as experience and circumstances shall dictate; constantly keeping in view that it is folly in one nation to look for disinterested favors from another; that it must pay with a portion of its independence for whatever it may accept under that character; that, by such acceptance, it may place itself in the condition of having given equivalents for nominal favors, and yet of being reproached with ingratitude for not giving more. There can be no greater error than to expect or calculate upon real favors from nation to nation. It is an illusion, which experience must cure, which a just pride ought to discard. . . .

How far in the discharge of my official duties I have been guided by the principles which have been delineated, the public records and other evidences of my conduct must witness to you and to the world. To myself, the assurance of my own conscience is, that I have at least believed myself to be guided by them. . . .

With me a predominant motive has been to endeavor to gain time to our country to settle and mature its yet recent institutions, and to progress without interruption to that degree of strength and consistency which is necessary to give it, humanly speaking, ***the command of its own fortunes***. . . .

United States
19th September, 1796
Geo. Washington"[172] (Emphasis added and reformatted.)

(I attached the entire transcribed speech as Addendum C of this book. The old English (1700's) language is a little different than we are now accustomed to reading, but it is very well-written. I suggest taking the time to read the entire treasured speech because it is from one of our nation's leading founding fathers, offers more guidance than I quote above, and is written with love for our nation.)

We looked at some history. Now, let's fast forward back to our present U.S. government.

Many of our nation's Congressional and Presidential actions have not been the will of the citizens or in the best interests of our sovereign nation. Many presidents of the United States of America and many members of our Congress have also been out of touch with our nation's citizens. Congress' and past presidents' culpability is seen by authorizing the Federal Reserve to be our nation's central bank, not ending the Federal Reserve, allowing financial chaos in markets, making illusionary financial markets by the Plunge Protection Team, allowing the Federal Reserve to even provide bailouts to foreign banks and corporations, agreeing to allow our nation's debt to grow to ridiculously large proportions, etc. (I think that many things that Congress and Presidents have done are not even known or understood by the citizens. For example, I think many citizens did not know that the Federal Reserve bailed out foreign corporations. At the same time, many people in foreign nations hate our nation.) Our nation's debt is at historic and critical levels. We are at a point that our nation's debt is a huge and growing bubble that is about to burst.

How can we proactively make changes to our U.S. national government in a peaceful manner?

As I explained earlier in this book, in the past, U.S. laws have gone back and forth on private central banking with only very temporary solutions. Of course, if we only make changes to our U.S. central banking to stop the Federal Reserve, Congress could easily change the laws back.

As you know, our nation has enormous debts. Also, our

U.S. debt is growing. If in one year, Congress balances the budget, in another year Congress could easily incur huge deficits again.

Therefore, it would be wise if some changes were made by Constitution <u>amendments</u> to fully cure our current economic problems and to prevent some future economic problems.

There are 2 ways to do a Constitutional Amendments (i.e., by the U.S. Congress or by a Convention of the States).

The **U.S. Constitution** states,

"**Article. V.**

The <u>Congress,</u> whenever two thirds of both Houses shall deem it necessary, shall propose Amendments to this Constitution, **or,**<u> on the Application of the Legislatures of two thirds of the several States,</u> **shall** <u>call a Convention for proposing Amendments, which, in either Case, shall be valid to all Intents and Purposes, as Part of this Constitution, when ratified by the Legislatures of three fourths of the several States, or by Conventions in three fourths thereof, as the one or the other Mode of Ratification may be proposed by the Congress;</u> Provided that no Amendment which may be made prior to the Year One thousand eight hundred and eight shall in any Manner affect the first and fourth Clauses in the Ninth Section of the first Article; and that no State, without its Consent, shall be deprived of its equal Suffrage in the Senate. . . ."[173]

The method of a convention to make U.S. Constitutional amendments by the states is known as a Constitutional Convention. A Constitutional Convention is also known as a Convention of the States.

The states' Constitutional Amendment powers are a pressure valve for the will of the U.S. citizens. The states' Constitutional amendment power is a way for U.S. citizens to make peaceful changes to government.

Clearly, some Constitutional amendments proposed by the states might be corrections that would even take power away from a runaway and overly powerful U.S. Congress.

I strongly believe that our Constitution needs to be amended to rein in the out of control Federal government that is ruining our nation.

Would Constitutional Amendments be easy? No.

People in power almost always want to keep power. This is usually true even if the people in power are ruining a nation. More, I believe this is true even if the great majority of the citizens are against the established people in power. Therefore, if a Constitutional Convention was sought by the states to makes changes to the Constitution, you could expect resistance by many of those already in power.

I believe that there are some people in power that really care about the citizens. I am also hopeful that there are some people in power that want some real changes to the Federal government and to state governments.

How can we tell if someone wants real change? Look at what they say about subject matters. More important, look at what they really did in the past. Congress has not passed Constitutional amendments or sufficient laws to correct our nation's economic problems. This is proof that most members of Congress do not really want changes in U.S. economics.

Some citizens may feel that they are scared of a runaway Constitutional Convention by the states. They might fear that such a Constitutional Convention by the states could make Constitutional amendments that would be hurtful and lead to a national crisis.

I assert the opposite. We are already in a national crisis. Clearly, our current Federal government is already out of control. As you know, our past U.S. Congress and past Presidents have created enormous U.S. debt levels and other terrible national problems. Therefore, we already have a runaway Federal government.

The states have the ability, and even the duty, to act to control the United States of America.

For example, the states have the powers of Constitutional amendments in order to allow the people to organize, unite and act to fix problems in our United States when a runaway U.S. Congress does not act according to the will of the people.

But, it is more. The states' power to make Constitutional amendments is a check on the power of Congress, the President, the U.S. Supreme Court, and the entire Federal government. Again, the states' Constitutional amendment power is a pressure valve for the U.S. citizens.

The states' ability to make Constitutional amendments is a way to have peaceful changes to government.

Even though we have Article V of the Constitution, there have been some disagreements on how states can start a convention to make amendments to our nation's Constitution.

For example, one way of contesting whether the states can have a Convention of the States to make Constitutional amendments involves whether there is enough number of states calling for a convention on a specific topic.

The Friends of the Article V Convention's (FOAVC) resourceful website states in pertinent part,

"While the legal and constitutional evidence is overwhelming that applications submitted by the states for an Article V Convention call are to be counted by a simple numeric count of applying states with no other terms or conditions, some believe Congress must first "aggregate" state applications by amendment subject matter within the application before it is obligated to call a convention. Thus, according to this theory, if Congress determines an insufficient number of applications on a specific amendment subject exist, Congress is not obligated to call a convention. This theory has never been tested in court. It is not supported by any legal or constitutional evidence either from the 1787 Convention, discussion by the Founders, discussion in Congress or by Supreme Court rulings. Despite the clear and unambiguous language of Article V ("Congress . . . shall call a convention to propose amendments on the application of two thirds of the several state legislatures) this theory holds Congress has the authority to refuse to call a convention unless conditions Congress defines and controls are satisfied. In sum, "same subject" advocates believe Congress has the right to veto the Constitution."[174] (Emphasis added.)

Again, Article V of the U.S. Constitution clearly uses words requiring that, "The Congress, . . . on the Application of the Legislatures of two thirds of the several States, shall call a Convention for proposing Amendments. . . ." The word "shall" shows that Congress does not have an option. Therefore, this subject matter argument is a very weak and incorrect.

Another argument against allowing the states to have a convention to make amendments to our Constitution involves a time limitation.

The Friends of the Article V Convention's (FOAVC) resourceful website also states,

> "Another untested, <u>unsupported theory</u> regarding counting applications is referred to as the "contemporaneous" theory. Some "same subject" advocates also argue applications also have a <u>contemporary limit</u> either because the state attaches one in the language of the application or because Congress can attach such limit."[175] (Emphasis added.)

The states seem to be hung up on asking Congress for permission to hold a Constitutional Convention. For example, in a 2014 article entitled, *34 States Call for Constitutional Convention — and Possible Rewrite*, Andrea Billups wrote,

> "Republican Rep. Duncan Hunter of California recently asked [Speaker of the U.S. House of Representatives (at the time) John] Boehner for clarification as to where the state count stands, and if Michigan has tipped the two-thirds majority needed to make the convention call.
>
> With the recent decision by Michigan lawmakers, it is important that the House — and those of us who support a balanced budget amendment — determine whether the necessary number of states have acted and the appropriate role of Congress should be in this case," Hunter wrote to Boehner. <u>Boehner spokesman Michael Steel told The Washington Times that the Republican leader will have his lawyers review the request</u>."[176] (Emphasis added.)

Don't hold your breath for Congress to get back to the people on Convention of the States issues to make Constitutional amendments.

If Congress wanted to make Constitutional amendments, they would do it themselves.

Why hasn't Congress acted?

I simply believe that almost all members of Congress do not want to make Constitutional amendments. I will explain more on this below.

In addition, almost all members of Congress do not understand that Congress has caused most of our U.S. economic problems by Congress' creation of a private (non-government) Federal Reserve, Congress' creation of our huge U.S. debt, Congress' deregulation of the banks, Congress not preparing our nation for the effect of technology on our economy, etc.

The influence of big money on U.S. politics is another reason that Congress will not act to amend the Constitution now.

I believe Congress won't do any Constitutional amendments until everything in our economy and nation completely crashes down.

The states should act now. The states should not wait until our nation is in an economic collapse and full crisis. The states should not wait until their citizens are terribly suffering.

Maybe, when the states get close to a Constitutional Convention, Congress will finally say that Congress will act to make Constitutional amendments. Congress will do this so Congress could control the wording and process of amendments to try to keep more Congressional power.

However, the states should not stop once the states start to make Constitutional changes even if Congress suddenly says it will make the changes. Once the states gather, the states should continue to be the ones to control and make the amendments.

Remember, a Convention of the States would probably involve Constitutional amendments to <u>limit Congress' powers</u> on U.S. debt and other huge issues.

Therefore, again, Congress clearly does not want Constitutional amendments. Congress does not want limits on its powers.

If the states' power with a Constitutional Convention could limit Congress' Constitutional powers, should the states have to seek permission from Congress in order to contemplate changes to the Constitution? No. That would make no sense.

Don't we trust our states as much as we trust Congress to do the simple math of keeping track of the how many states are asking for a Convention of the States? I do!

We should trust our states more than our Federal government. I somewhat trust the checks and balances of our governments. But, even with checks and balances, I believe any governments can be manipulated into oligarchies. As I previously wrote in this book, I believe many parts of our U.S. government have already become an oligarchy.

I trust my State of Wisconsin government more than I trust our Federal government because: my state government is geographically closer to me, I have a more proportionally valuable vote with my state government, my state government is not as influenced by large financial lobbyists, my state government is much less fiscally and administratively out of control when compared to the Federal government, I have more contact with my state government, my state government is smaller, I have more control in my state government, my state elected officials live in my state, etc.

A Hamline Law Review article entitled *Lawful and Peaceful Revolution: Article V and Congress' Present Duty to*

Call a Convention for Proposing Amendments by The Honorable Bruce M. Van Sickle and Lynn M. Boughey, states,

> "*We do **not** believe . . . that Congress has the power to control the [Constitution Convention] process in any way*. . . . *The decisive defect in [the position that Congress has the power to set procedures that govern calling a Constitutional Convention] and in the proposed legislation attempting to <u>control and limit</u> the convention is that it <u>exceeds by far the authority of Congress to legislate in this area</u>. Congress <u>only</u> possesses the authority granted to it by the Constitution.*"[177] (Emphasis added.)

Since Congress does not control the states' Constitutional Convention process in any way, the states should not need permission from Congress for the states to start a Constitutional Convention.

Clearly, the United States of America is group of the member states that are *united*, hence the "*United*" "*States*" of America.

The citizens of the United States of America ultimately makeup our government because we are a Republic. Remember, we are a republic government *of, by, and for* the people.

We know that the Constitution already has a process for the states to make amendments to the United States Constitution. How should states go ahead and make applications for a Constitutional Convention?

States shouldn't ask for a Constitutional Convention. States should just demand a Constitutional Convention after a few things are done.

First, the states should each a pass laws indicating: The

State of _____, hereby enacts and applies for a Constitutional Convention by the states, and hereby provides full and complete authority for the governor, or for any delegate as the governor may assign within the governor's sole discretion, to draft, create, vote and/or decide upon <u>any and all amendments</u> to the U.S. Constitution (according to Article V of the U.S. Constitution) that the governor, or governor's delegate, deems necessary and appropriate within the governor's, or governor's delegate's, sole discretion. This authority allows the governor, or governor's delegate, to set and/or agree upon any and all date(s), time(s) and place(s) for such Constitutional Convention by the states within the next 7 years. If a new governor is elected in this state during this 7 year period, the new governor, or for any delegate as the new governor may assign within the new governor's sole discretion, is authorized to replace the previous governor and/or previous governor's delegate in any Constitutional Convention, and shall have the same full and complete authority as indicated above. (A model language should be broadly and powerful drafted to enable the states to amend the Constitution despite anyone's attempted argument that the Convention did not have the authority from the states. The States would also be wise to enact the same language and time period to avoid any arguments. Model language used should be shared with all the States. The actual and exact model language is beyond the scope of this book.)

Second, citizens and the states are free to talk about Constitutional ideas and should communicate. States should each communicate with each other about which states will be willing to attend such a proposed convention and what amendments the states want to the U.S. Constitution. Coincidentally, States could use technology for good to facilitate this communication. Again, the states should and can communicate. To the states in the United States, I say: "Pick up a phone, write an email, use video conferencing, and somehow communicate with each other." Then, the states should just send delegates to meet informally, <u>without permission from Congress</u>, and start to talk. (The responsibility of such convention members is high, and only those people that have voices of the highest integrity should be sent to such a meeting.)

Third, when enough states' governors/delegates have actually physically gathered (at least 34 states) in attendance at the informal meeting, the states should immediately send Congress notice signed by all the states governors/delegates that those states are applying for amendments via an Article V Constitutional Convention and the states are calling for a Constitutional Convention. (Again, since Article V of the U.S. Constitution clearly states that, "The Congress, . . . on the Application of the Legislatures of two thirds of the several States, *shall* call a Convention for proposing Amendments. . . .," Congress must officially call the Constitutional Convention of the states. If Congress does not call a Constitutional Convention of the states after Congress receives the 34 states' applications, each state could inform their state's citizens of Congress' refusal. In addition, the states could also protest by keeping delegates at a Constitutional Convention site until the Constitutional Convention of the states is started. Most important, if Congress does not call a Constitutional Convention of the states after Congress receives the 34 states' applications, a Constitutional crisis would result and the states would probably seek an immediate U.S. Supreme court decision in the states' favor.) Then, the states can just start the Constitutional Convention and formally decide what amendments should be made to the Constitution. (I do not need to emphasize the need for amendments. I am even making suggestions for Constitutional amendments later in this book. But, of course, the Convention of States will decide on which Constitutional amendments to propose. At the same time, I hope I do not need to emphasize the need for any amendments to be well-reasoned and meant only for the benefit of the nation as a whole.

So, states can do amendments to our U.S. Constitution according to the procedure in our Constitution. What types of amendments should the states make to our Constitution?

I have my own ideas of what Constitutional Amendments we should have to solve our nation's problems.

HERE ARE MY KAFKAS' TOP 2 SUGGESTIONS FOR CONSTITUTIONAL AMENDMENTS:

1. **Only the U.S. Treasury shall be the Federal Government's central bank.** Our government can and should make its own credit and do its own banking. We will owe no one anything and we will really be a free nation. (If I get one idea out to people by this book, I hope it is that our own government needs to absolutely and fully take over our own government's central banking. Our government can lend money to many small credit unions and many small banks that will loan money to many people and many businesses. We also need to have full checks and balances on our central banking. In addition, we need complete and constant transparency of our central banking.)

2. **The U.S. government shall have a balanced budget each year unless a law allowing the unbalanced budget for that specific year is passed by 2/3 votes of the U.S. Congress, 2/3 votes of the states' governors, and the U.S. President.** (I would also add: If the President vetoes, ¾ of Congress and ¾ of the states' governors will be required to overturn the president's veto.)

The United States of America has big problems. We need big solutions. Therefore, I strongly believe the Constitutional Amendments I listed should be passed.

I discussed suggested U.S. Constitutional Amendments above. Next, I make suggestions for U.S. laws.

We need to make laws to stimulate the number of people employed, fund our nation, get rid of our huge national debt, and adjust to technology for the betterment of our nation and

168

our citizens. We also need to limit some very risky technologies that could harm our nation and economy.

HERE ARE MY <u>KAFKAS' TOP 30 SUGGESTIONS FOR</u> U.S. <u>**LAWS**</u>:

1. **Re-establish and broaden the Glass–Steagall Act to prevent commercial banks from doing investment banking.**

2. **Stop Derivatives.** (We need to completely stop the risky derivatives financial markets.)

3. **Stop the Plunge Protection Team.** (We need real and fair stock markets that are not manipulated by the Plunge Protection Team.)

4. **Don't do any more Bailouts of the Banks and Financial Institutions.** (We must protect our nation. We should not protect the rich, the banks and the corporations. Mortgage insurance is different. We can keep mortgage insurance.)

5. **Change the U.S. Dept. of Labor wage and hour regulations so that there would be no classification of employees that would be exempt from overtime pay (only self-employed would be exempt). Also, make overtime three times the rate of pay so that employers will want to hire more workers instead of paying overtime.** (As technology leverages the amount of work that employees can do, there is less need for employees. We need to reasonably adjust and spread out the job work so that more people are employed. Will there be business, labor and political resistance to this suggestion? Yes. But, if the entire economy fully collapses, no one will be working! If more people are working, there will be fewer foreclosures, less crime, fewer divorces, etc. It will be better for the United States' macro-economy for more people to be working

fewer hours with the leverage of technology, than to have fewer people working overtime. The United States' macro-economy affects everyone in the U.S. and even affects the world. If too many people are out of work in the U.S., the macro-economy will be negatively affected by the employment supply bubble. Technological advances increases productivity and not as many employees are needed. If technology increases and we adjust the wage and hour regulations, the U.S. will now be able to produce even more than it has in the past with the increased technology it has now. More importantly, the U.S. employed people (consumers) will be able to buy more products. What reasons are there for employees with good salaried jobs to want to change overtime laws? These people could have more time with their families, more recreational time, more time to do positive volunteer work for charities, and/or time to start their own side businesses (self-employment) on days off of work. Other changes to wage and hour regulations will be needed in the future. For example, with continued increases in technology, someday a 4 day/work week might eventually become a part of the macro-economic solution. This might be more appropriate and popularly acceptable to fully consider 20-30 years from now. (Hopefully, the entire macro-economy won't crash before this is needed.) But, for now, the other changes in the overtime laws and other suggested solutions should be enough *if* implemented quickly enough.)

6. **Increase the minimum wage for employees in companies that are making large <u>profits</u> (not gross income) over $1,000,000.**

7. **Decrease hours that <u>children</u> are allowed to work.** (Children should be concentrating on school and other youth activities. Children should not work more than 1 day per week during the school year, not at all during exam times, and only 2 days per week in the summer.)

8. **Create large tax credits to any companies hiring and retaining new employees for 1 year or more in certain areas.** (The areas of new employment should be strategically well-reasoned so that the U.S.A. will become a world leader in clean and safe energy; information/computers; cyber security; medicine; science; physics; space; parks; education; environmental clean-up, environmental sustainability, food safety; crop and land sustainability; organic foods by utilizing safe alternatives to pesticides and herbicides; alternatives to genetically modified organisms (GMOs); clean water; water sustainability; recycling; national defense/security; and other advanced technologies. At the same time, decrease tax credits in many other areas so that the business focus will be on using the tax credits that will increase employment in strategic areas.

9. **Change unemployment insurance to include longer terms of unemployment benefits.** (Also, change unemployment insurance to include incentives for unemployed people to receive additional education and training in the strategic areas mentioned above.

10. **Make New Deal #2.** (Create temporary government sponsors jobs that actually benefit public works, public parks and public services. These temporary jobs should put a large number of citizens to work in the United States of America. Again, if anyone says that we should not invest in a New Deal #2, ask them if they supported the unforgettable bank and corporate bailouts?)

11. **Increase the number of people in AmeriCorps and Peace Corps.** (This will help the U.S.A, help build good will with other nations, help with international trade, and to decrease U.S. unemployment. More, other nations will want to become more like the U.S.A. which will make trade and the world more stable.)

12. **Increase grants and low-interest student loans for people to gain advanced education in strategic areas mentioned above.** (Also, provide that a reasonable amount of student loans may be more easily reduced for public service and some non-profit jobs. Help more non-profits and graduates to become aware of student loan forgiveness for public service. Prices at many states' public universities have skyrocketed. At the state legislative levels, many states should substantially decrease state public universities' tuition and student dorm housing.)

13. **Government public service employees should only have reasonable salaries. In addition, the Federal, state and local governments should not allow retired employees to take a government pension and then return to their past government jobs as paid temporary or permanent employees (i.e., double-dipping).** (Some government employees make unreasonably high salaries.[178] I have also seen double-dipping multiple times in the State of Wisconsin government. If someone retires from a government job and they want to continue to work, they could work for a private business, volunteer or start their own business. There is no reason for this type of double-dipping with two government checks relating to the same government (i.e., government retirement checks and government work paychecks) while there is a large supply of potential employees that want and need a job. If there is ever a rare reason to allow double-dipping, it should be a big enough reason that a governor must authorize the specific employee in the state government job or the secretary of the U.S. department must authorize the employee in the Federal job, AND make a public announcements.)

14. **When a government contract proposal is considered for anything using Federal money, a criteria should include how many people will work in a project and**

what work skills the employees will have or learn, and how many people that were previously unemployed will be hired for his project. (Notice for these projects should include strong affirmative action to hire unemployed citizens. Notices of the affirmative action for hiring unemployed citizens should be included in the job advertising and announcements.)

15. We should increase income taxes upon the very wealthy individuals with caveats. (Once someone makes above a very large amount, just for example $100,000,000/yr., the super wealthy person should be taxed at a heavier percent like 50% – but still encouraged to make and keep more money. This high income tax is because whoever is making this huge money is using the roads, communications, technology, people educated through public schools, and/or other infrastructure of our nation. At the same time, with the incentive of large tax credits, we should encourage wealthy individuals and corporations to hire more people and to make donations to actual public service non-profits. We should eliminate many current tax credits allowed to the wealthy (although other credits should be still allowed to those that are not super wealthy) so that wealthy will want to take advantage of the above tax credits.)

16. The Social Security program should have no maximum limits on the amount of income that is taxed. (According to the U.S. government Social Security Website, "Social Security's Old-Age, Survivors, and Disability Insurance (OASDI) program limits the amount of earnings subject to taxation for a given year. The same annual limit also applies when those earnings are used in a benefit computation. This limit changes each year with changes in the national average wage index. We call this annual limit the contribution and benefit base. For earnings in 2017, this base is $127,200."[179] Therefore, according to this Website, the

wealthy currently do not pay Social Security tax on all of their income. The Social Security program should have no maximum limits on the amount of income that is taxed. With this suggested change, wealthy would pay more Social Security tax. For example, millionaires and billionaires would pay Social Security tax on all of their income. This will increase the Social Security fund and make the fund much safer and secure for future generations.)

17. **Tax-exempt (non-profit) hospitals and other entities should have limitations on the salary amounts/compensations paid to executives.** (Executives of nonprofits should not make more than $500,000.00/yr. salaries. Tax-exempt hospitals should also have requirements to reduce outstanding accounts for medical bills for people with low-incomes when the patients do not have health insurance or enough money to pay their large out-of-pocket insurance deductibles and/or insurance co-pays. (However, our U.S. and state governments should stay away from any control of, and should stay away from taxing, religious institutions. I personally feel that clergy should not be clergy for the money. But, trying to regulate religious institutions is a very dangerous and slippery road that must be completely avoided.)

18. **Quickly phase-out the nuclear power plants that have any reasonable potential risk. Also increase safeguards for, and encourage cost-effective clean energy alternatives to, nuclear power plants.** (Nuclear power plant reactor tragedies such as 3-Mile Island, Chernobyl, Japan's Fukushima, etc., need to be prevented. If a private company has a nuclear accident or disaster, the company should be ready and able to pay for all damages caused by the accident or disaster. We should also increase tort liabilities, insurance requirements, regulatory compliance requirements, and minimal assets of companies that invest in risky energies

such as nuclear power that could damage large portions of our world permanently or even end our world. If we are thinking that nuclear power would be a part of the solution to our macro-economic problems, we should keep thinking. A nuclear reactor disaster could negatively affect our entire macro-economy. Worse, a nuclear power plant accident could kill many people and cause injuries for many generations. For now, I would even rather have clean coal than nuclear.)

19. **Encourage clean energy inventions and innovations.** (Here is just a few ideas: We should establish a public contest to be held every seven (7) years to find the best safe, clean and renewable energy technology available with a few very large Federal government monetary prizes (tax free) and other honorary recognition (such as a honorary metals). The government should also provide publicity and broadcast the contest for the winner. This will get the best scientists, engineers and others working in their businesses, labs, kitchen tables, garages, etc. We never know where this idea will come from and it should be sought with the public interest in mind. The grand prize and the top two runner-up contest winners submissions all should become public domain (free for anyone to use) in the U.S.A. only. The rest could be patented for sale and commercial use (if patentable) as the market allows. Why is a contest needed by the government? We can't wait any longer. For many years, the private market is not working well for energy inventions. Many people wonder if a new clean energy invention was already found, but it was somehow boxed and put on a shelf so that wealth and power could be maintained by owners of other energy sources. (For example, the oil industry is largely run by a powerful oligopoly.) What are some other reasons for such a contest? Such a contest would be a sound investment in our economy, environment, political stability and our children's future. This type of contest would also reduce our nation's reliance on foreign

energy resources. A new clean energy invention would eventually create new jobs as the United States re-tools. In addition, these new ideas will make our country a world-leader in business and good technology. Initially, only U.S. businesses should be able to reasonably sell this new technology and/or products from this new technology to other countries. Such a prize might sound like a waste of lot of money. However, as I explained earlier in this book, we are trying to solve macro-economic problems including a huge U.S.A. Debt. (If anyone says that we should not invest in finding a safe, clean, renewable energy source, ask them if they supported the huge bank bailouts?) I would add that a company that already has a secret invention for clean energy (that is not patented) would have the ability to bring this invention forward during this contest. These are just a few ideas on how to encourage new clean energy inventions. We need to keep trying to think of new ways to stimulate new clean energy inventions for the future.)

20. **Increase government funding for environmental clean-up of water, air and land from all types of pollution.** (This is a good way to get people working and to clean up the United States' environment at the same time.)

21. **Ban genetically modified organisms (GMOs) in food and crops completely until further and <u>full consideration</u> is completed.** (Technology is moving faster than critical analysis of the technology. A full discussion is beyond the topic of this book. However, GMOs could affect, or even be a disaster to, our entire world's web of life! There are some things which require the full consideration of many scientific, health, environmental, economic, legal, moral, ethical, spiritual and other issues.)

22. **Require that all GMO products have large and clear**

labels that state that the products contain GMO ingredients. (Some products might not be food or crops. In addition, some products might come from other nations. This law is also a way for people to choose to stop eating GMO foods if the above law banning GMOs is not fully created.)

23. **Ban genetic splicing of any species.** (We need to protect our human species and other species. Again, technology is moving faster than critical analysis of the technology and a full discussion is beyond the topic of this book. However, some genetic splicing is intuitively wrong. For example, "Researchers from the University of Wyoming have developed a way to incorporate spiders' silk-spinning genes into goats, allowing the researchers to harvest the silk protein from the goats' milk for a variety of applications."[180] Again, there are some things which require the full consideration of many spiritual, ethical, moral, health, safety, environmental and other issues.)

24. **Provide an immediate investigation and analysis by a team of diverse scientists on whether we should support and/or allow particle acceleration projects.** (Many people are concerned that this could devastate our world.)

25. **Provide an immediate investigation by a team of diverse scientists with no connections to the fluoride or water bottling industry on whether fluoride should be allowed in our nation's water supply.** (Many people are concerned that fluoride could be harmful.)

26. **Provide an immediate investigation by a team of diverse scientists with no connections to the pharmaceutical industry on the safety of vaccinations.** (There are many public concerns about vaccinations. We need a healthy people to have a

healthy national economy. More importantly, this is the right thing to do.)

27. **Provide financial support and tax credits for some backup Pre-Industrial Age and Industrial Age skills with some tax credits to low/moderate income individual workers who do "old labor." We also need to provide financial support and tax credits to people who write books on these subjects.** (We need to support these skills so these skills are preserved for our country in case these skills are needed in the future because of any type of technological catastrophe.)

28. **Provide financial support and tax credits for some organic foods grown in the U.S.A. We also need to provide financial support and tax credits to people who write books on these subjects.** (Some people know ways to naturally limit many types of pests and diseases to plants and crops. We need to support these skills for the current generation and so these skills are preserved for our future nation.)

29. **Prevent illegal immigration and secure our borders.** (Simply, illegal immigration is different than legal immigration. For economic, crime prevention and military/national security reasons, we need to know who is coming into the U.S.A. Likewise, we need to know what is coming into the U.S.A.)

30. **All election computer systems, electronic ballots, election technology, and any other election machines must be fully owned, managed and run by the State and local governments (not by private companies and not by the Federal government).** (Again, we have a government by the people. Our republic needs to be controlled by ONLY our citizens. We need to keep the decentralization of power within the U.S.A. The more national elections are locally controlled, the less chance of widespread systematic

fraud. Also, no United Nations, no foreign governments, and no private companies may be used in any way to control and/or manage our elections.)

Above, I made some suggestions for solutions via U.S. Constitutional amendments and new U.S. laws. We need to carefully examine what Constitutional amendments and laws we should make in the United States.

What about the state and local governments?

The state and local governments will also need to be more vigilant and fiscally responsible. The states are accustomed to getting the Federal money for many programs. If the U.S. economy collapses, or if the U.S. government becomes more fiscally and monetarily responsible to prevent a collapse, the state and local governments will probably not get as much money from the U.S. government. Therefore, the state and local governments will have to do more for their own residents with their own state and local government revenues.

For example, state and local governments should change how they spend money on sports arenas and stadiums. In the past, state and local governments have provided very large amounts of money towards sports arenas and/or stadiums. The owners of many sports entertainment teams are billionaires and do not need government money. I have seen a city that had a current basketball arena in excellent functioning condition and beautiful, yet state and local governments provided many hundreds of millions of dollars for a new arena. Government tax money should not be used for new sports arenas or stadiums that benefit privately owned sports teams. More, higher priorities exist in states such as helping homeless children, homeless adults, poor, unemployed, children in low-income families, disabled, blighted communities, clean water, education, law enforcement, firefighters and EMTs, next generation job technology, safe parks, community centers, roads, mass transit, etc. Some will argue that a new arena will bring more jobs. But, any business can claim that if the state and local governments provide hundreds of millions of dollars to help support a private business, it will bring jobs.

I provided some suggestions that I believe would help our nation.

You might be saying to yourself, I am just one person, what can I do?

In general, I believe we all should try to <u>personally take 3 steps</u> to save our economy and to save our nation:

1. We need to get real information. But, don't trust the media just because it is big, on TV, or because it has been around for a long time. Many people believe that a lot of news is biased and unreliable. In addition, I believe that some news medias are intentionally producing fake news. More, I believe that some news medias are not covering important news. I also believe that some big news medias are part of the oligarchy. I suggest citizens look deeper into issues instead of just hearing sound bites. Do your own research. If you find that a news media is not telling the truth, find news that you can trust. Question everything in the news. You have freedom. Make up your own minds.

2. We need to be active. You might have heard people say, "Don't talk about politics or religion." I say the opposite. For example, we should try to talk to each other (i.e., your family, friends and neighbors) about government and politics. By respectfully talking with each other, we learn and collaborate. So, I think it is important to talk in a civilized manner when we are able to communicate with people and the people want to communicate. (But, of course, I think it is important for everyone to use common sense and to stay clear of people that could be harmful.) We should also try to be active in our government since we "the people" are the government. For example, we need to try to think of

solutions for our nation. I hope some good comes out of this book for the U.S.A. But, if someone has better suggestions to solve our nation's economic crisis, great! But, great ideas won't solve anything unless some people start to take action. Therefore, we should vote. More, we should call, email and write to our elected officials and ask them to do what we want them to do. We could also write to newspapers and blogs. In addition, we desperately need more good and honest people to serve in government. Too often, no one runs for office and the same stagnant or corrupt people get reelected over and over. Therefore, if public service is a fit for people, it would be fantastic if more regular people ran for election of government offices. Likewise, we should be good citizens, respect the authority of our police, thank those in our military and veterans, try to help those in public service, etc. Another idea is to buy locally grown fresh and healthy produce when possible. This supports a great part of our economy. More, when shopping, make a routine of not using self-checkout lines run by computers. Instead, use checkout lines with real people. (And, don't forget to smile because life involves relationships with other people.) Furthermore, we should try to help all people (regardless of color, religion, sex, etc.) outside of the government. Volunteers are awesome! In summary, I suggest that we all are "activists" for good governments and good communities.

3. I believe that we should really pray to God. I believe that this is the most important step.

God is all knowing, all powerful, and can do anything.

The founding fathers of our nation established our nation under God.

I believe our nation was richly blessed because it was a nation under God.

For example, as I wrote earlier, the Declaration of Independence of the United States of America includes,

"We hold these truths to be self-evident, that all men are created equal, that they are endowed by their **Creator** with certain unalienable Rights, that among these are Life, Liberty and the pursuit of Happiness.--That to secure these rights, Governments are instituted among Men, deriving their just powers from the consent of the governed. . . ."[181] (Emphasis added.) (Again, the U.S. Declaration of Independence is so important that I have included a transcript of it as an appendix.)

George Washington also referred to religion in his Farewell Address.

Pull out a dollar bill from your wallet or purse. What do you see? On the back of our U.S. $1 bill, our country emphasizes, "**IN GOD WE TRUST.**"

Almost all citizens know the U.S. Pledge of Allegiance. Earlier in this book, I wrote about the importance of another aspect of our United States' *Pledge of Allegiance to the Flag.* A United States of America government website provides that our nation's *Pledge of Allegiance to the Flag* is as follows,

"I PLEDGE ALLEGIANCE TO THE FLAG OF THE UNITED STATES OF AMERICA AND TO THE REPUBLIC FOR WHICH IT STANDS, **ONE NATION UNDER GOD**, INDIVISIBLE, WITH LIBERTY AND JUSTICE FOR ALL."[182] (Emphasis added.)

There are many other examples of the importance of God in U.S. government and U.S. history.

What should we pray to God?

182

I suggest that we pray to God asking for guidance, help, peace, mercy and blessings for the United States of America and the world.

As societies develop more technology, it is clear that we have gained some knowledge. Of course, we do not know everything.

It is important to understand that knowledge and wisdom are not the same.

More, has society as a whole gained wisdom? I don't think so. We might have even lost some wisdom.

We need to take a step down from our illusionary pedestal. We don't know the best and wisest things to do for our nation.

I encourage our nation's leaders and <u>all</u> people to pray to God and remember to,

> "**<u>Trust in the Lord</u> with all thine heart; and lean not unto thine own understanding.**
>
> **In all thy ways acknowledge him, and he shall direct thy paths.**"
> Proverbs 3:5-6 King James Version (KJV) Holy Bible.[183] (Emphasis added.)

In addition, I encourage everyone to remember that,

> "Then one of them, which was a lawyer, asked him a question, tempting him, and saying,
>
> [']Master, which is the great commandment in the law?[']
>
> Jesus said unto him, [']***Thou shalt love the Lord***

__thy God with all thy heart, and with all thy__
__soul, and with all thy mind.__

__This is the first and great commandment.__

__And the second is like unto it, Thou shalt love__
__thy neighbour as thyself.__

__On these two commandments hang all the law__
__and the prophets.__[']"
Matthew 22:35-40 King James Version (KJV) Holy
Bible.[184] (Emphasis added.)

I believe we should love everyone in the world.

God loves us and knows what is best for us.

Even on just a logical basis, we must know that if we
don't love each other, all the technology advances will
eventually be used for bad reasons. More, if we don't love
each other, all the possible good government changes and all
the good world relations, will quickly disintegrate.

But, I believe we can't do it on our own and we need
God to really love each other.

The values and freedoms in the U.S.A. are what made
this nation great. These values were largely reflected in our
Constitution. Our U.S. Constitution is great, and we can also
improve it.

We still have a strong and sovereign nation.

However, I believe the United States is in jeopardy of a
historic, terrible, economic crisis.

I don't want to lose this great nation to another page in
history.

Certainly, when the United States of America is truly one nation under God, I know that we will be amazingly blessed by God.

In this book, I analyzed our nation's economic crisis and I suggested some solutions that I believe will help to save our nation.

Before it is too late for our nation, what do you think are the solutions?

What will you, "the people," do to save our nation?

ADDENDUM A

U.S. DECLARATION OF INDEPENDENCE

"Declaration of Independence: A Transcription

Note: The following text is a transcription of the Stone Engraving of the parchment Declaration of Independence (the document on display in the Rotunda at the National Archives Museum.) The spelling and punctuation reflects the original.

In Congress, July 4, 1776.

The unanimous Declaration of the thirteen united States of America, When in the Course of human events, it becomes necessary for one people to dissolve the political bands which have connected them with another, and to assume among the powers of the earth, the separate and equal station to which the Laws of Nature and of Nature's God entitle them, a decent respect to the opinions of mankind requires that they should declare the causes which impel them to the separation.

We hold these truths to be self-evident, that all men are created equal, that they are endowed by their Creator with certain unalienable Rights, that among these are Life, Liberty and the pursuit of Happiness.--That to secure these rights, Governments are instituted among Men, deriving their just powers from the consent of the governed, --That whenever any Form of Government becomes destructive of these ends, it is the Right of the People to alter or to abolish it, and to institute new Government, laying its foundation on such principles and organizing its powers in such form, as to them shall seem most likely to effect their Safety and Happiness. Prudence, indeed, will dictate that Governments long established should not be changed for light and transient causes; and accordingly all experience hath shewn, that mankind are more disposed to suffer, while evils are sufferable, than to right themselves by abolishing the forms to which they are accustomed. But when a long train of abuses and usurpations, pursuing invariably the same Object evinces a design to reduce them under absolute Despotism, it is their right, it is their duty, to throw off such Government, and to provide new Guards for their future security.--Such has been the patient sufferance of these Colonies; and such is now the necessity which constrains them to alter their former Systems of Government. The history of the present King of Great Britain is a history of repeated injuries and usurpations, all having in direct object the establishment of an absolute Tyranny over these States. To prove this, let Facts be submitted to a candid world.

He has refused his Assent to Laws, the most wholesome and necessary for the public good.

He has forbidden his Governors to pass Laws of immediate and pressing importance, unless suspended in their operation till his Assent should be obtained; and when so suspended, he has utterly neglected to attend to them.

He has refused to pass other Laws for the accommodation of large districts of people, unless those people would relinquish the right of Representation in the Legislature, a right inestimable to them and formidable to tyrants only.

He has called together legislative bodies at places unusual, uncomfortable, and distant from the depository of their public Records, for the sole purpose of fatiguing them into compliance with his measures.

He has dissolved Representative Houses repeatedly, for opposing with manly firmness his invasions on the rights of the people.

He has refused for a long time, after such dissolutions, to cause others to be elected; whereby the Legislative powers, incapable of Annihilation, have returned to the People at large for their exercise; the State remaining in the mean time exposed to all the dangers of invasion from without, and convulsions within.

He has endeavoured to prevent the population of these States; for that purpose obstructing the Laws for Naturalization of Foreigners; refusing to pass others to encourage their migrations hither, and raising the conditions of new Appropriations of Lands.

He has obstructed the Administration of Justice, by refusing his Assent to Laws for establishing Judiciary powers.

He has made Judges dependent on his Will alone, for the tenure of their offices, and the amount and payment of their salaries.

He has erected a multitude of New Offices, and sent hither swarms of Officers to harrass our people, and eat out their substance.

He has kept among us, in times of peace, Standing Armies without the Consent of our legislatures.

He has affected to render the Military independent of and superior to the Civil power.

He has combined with others to subject us to a jurisdiction foreign to our constitution, and unacknowledged by our laws; giving his Assent to their Acts of pretended Legislation:

For Quartering large bodies of armed troops among us:

For protecting them, by a mock Trial, from punishment for any Murders which they should commit on the Inhabitants of these States:

For cutting off our Trade with all parts of the world:

For imposing Taxes on us without our Consent:

For depriving us in many cases, of the benefits of Trial by Jury:

For transporting us beyond Seas to be tried for pretended offences

For abolishing the free System of English Laws in a neighbouring Province, establishing therein an Arbitrary government, and enlarging its Boundaries so as to render it at once an example and fit instrument for introducing the same absolute rule into these Colonies:

For taking away our Charters, abolishing our most valuable Laws, and altering fundamentally the Forms of our Governments:

For suspending our own Legislatures, and declaring themselves invested with power to legislate for us in all cases whatsoever.

He has abdicated Government here, by declaring us out of his Protection and waging War against us.

He has plundered our seas, ravaged our Coasts, burnt our towns, and destroyed the lives of our people.

He is at this time transporting large Armies of foreign Mercenaries to compleat the works of death, desolation and tyranny, already begun with circumstances of Cruelty & perfidy scarcely paralleled in the most barbarous ages, and totally unworthy the Head of a civilized nation.

He has constrained our fellow Citizens taken Captive on the high Seas to bear Arms against their Country, to become the executioners of their friends and Brethren, or to fall themselves by their Hands.

He has excited domestic insurrections amongst us, and has endeavoured to bring on the Inhabitants of our frontiers, the merciless Indian Savages, whose known rule of warfare, is an undistinguished destruction of all ages, sexes and conditions.

In every stage of these Oppressions We have Petitioned for Redress in the most humble terms: Our repeated Petitions have been answered only by repeated injury. A Prince whose character is thus marked by every act which may define a Tyrant, is unfit to be the ruler of a free people.

Nor have We been wanting in attentions to our Brittish brethren. We have warned them from time to time of attempts by their legislature to extend an unwarrantable jurisdiction over us. We have reminded them of the circumstances of our emigration and settlement here. We have appealed to their native justice and magnanimity, and we have conjured them by the ties of our common kindred to disavow these usurpations, which, would inevitably interrupt our connections and correspondence. They too have been deaf to the voice of justice and of consanguinity. We must, therefore, acquiesce in the necessity, which denounces our Separation, and hold them, as we hold the rest of mankind, Enemies in War, in Peace Friends.

We, therefore, the Representatives of the united States of America, in General Congress, Assembled, appealing to the Supreme Judge of the world for the rectitude of our intentions, do, in the Name, and by Authority of the good People of these Colonies, solemnly publish and declare, That these United Colonies are, and of Right ought to be Free and Independent States; that they are Absolved from all Allegiance to the British Crown, and that all political connection between them and the State of Great Britain, is and ought to be totally dissolved; and that as Free and Independent States, they have full Power to levy War, conclude Peace, contract Alliances, establish Commerce, and to do all other Acts and Things which Independent States may of right do. And for the support of this Declaration, with a firm reliance on the protection of divine Providence, we mutually pledge to each other our Lives, our Fortunes and our sacred Honor.

Georgia

Button Gwinnett Lyman Hall George Walton

North Carolina

William Hooper Joseph Hewes John Penn

South Carolina

Edward Rutledge Thomas Heyward, Jr. Thomas Lynch, Jr. Arthur Middleton

Massachusetts

John Hancock

Maryland

Samuel Chase William Paca Thomas Stone Charles Carroll of Carrollton

Virginia

George Wythe Richard Henry Lee Thomas Jefferson Benjamin Harrison Thomas Nelson, Jr. Francis Lightfoot Lee Carter Braxton

Pennsylvania

Robert Morris Benjamin Rush Benjamin Franklin John Morton George Clymer James Smith George Taylor James Wilson George Ross"[185] (Reformatted.)

ADDENDUM B

U.S. CONSTITUTION, BILL OF RIGHTS & OTHER AMENDMENTS

"The Constitution of the United States: A Transcription

*Note: The following text is a transcription of the **Constitution** as it was inscribed by Jacob Shallus on parchment (the document on display in the Rotunda at the National Archives Museum.) The spelling and punctuation reflects the original.*

'***We the People of the United States***, in Order to form a more perfect Union, establish Justice, insure domestic Tranquility, provide for the common defence, promote the general Welfare, and secure the Blessings of Liberty to ourselves and our Posterity, do ordain and establish this Constitution for the United States of America.

Article. I.

Section. 1.

All legislative Powers herein granted shall be vested in a Congress of the United States, which shall consist of a Senate and House of Representatives.

Section. 2.

The House of Representatives shall be composed of Members chosen every second Year by the People of the several States, and the Electors in each State shall have the Qualifications requisite for Electors of the most numerous Branch of the State Legislature.

No Person shall be a Representative who shall not have attained to the Age of twenty five Years, and been seven Years a Citizen of the United States, and who shall not, when elected, be an Inhabitant of that State in which he shall be chosen.

Representatives and direct Taxes shall be apportioned among the several States which may be included within this Union, according to their respective Numbers, which shall be determined by adding to the whole Number of free Persons, including those bound to Service for a Term of Years, and excluding Indians not taxed, three fifths of all other Persons. The actual Enumeration shall be made within three Years after the first Meeting of the Congress of the United States, and within every subsequent Term of ten Years, in such Manner as they shall by Law direct. The Number of Representatives shall not exceed one for every thirty Thousand, but each State shall have at Least one Representative; and until such enumeration shall be made, the State of New Hampshire shall be entitled to chuse three, Massachusetts eight, Rhode-Island and Providence Plantations one, Connecticut five, New-York six, New Jersey four, Pennsylvania eight, Delaware one, Maryland six, Virginia ten, North Carolina five, South Carolina five, and Georgia three.

When vacancies happen in the Representation from any State, the Executive Authority thereof shall issue Writs of Election to fill such Vacancies.

The House of Representatives shall chuse their Speaker and other Officers; and shall have the sole Power of Impeachment.

Section. 3.

The Senate of the United States shall be composed of two Senators from each State, chosen by the Legislature thereof, for six Years; and each Senator shall have one Vote.

Immediately after they shall be assembled in Consequence of the first Election, they shall be divided as equally as may be into three Classes. The Seats of the Senators of the first Class shall be vacated at the Expiration of the second Year, of the second Class at the Expiration of the fourth Year, and of the third Class at the Expiration of the sixth Year, so that one third may be chosen every second Year; and if Vacancies happen by Resignation, or otherwise, during the Recess of the Legislature of any State, the Executive thereof may make temporary Appointments until the next Meeting of the Legislature, which shall then fill such Vacancies.

No Person shall be a Senator who shall not have attained to the Age of thirty Years, and been nine Years a Citizen of the United States, and who shall not, when elected, be an Inhabitant of that State for which he shall be chosen.

The Vice President of the United States shall be President of the Senate, but shall have no Vote, unless they be equally divided.

The Senate shall chuse their other Officers, and also a President pro tempore, in the Absence of the Vice President, or when he shall exercise the Office of President of the United States.

The Senate shall have the sole Power to try all Impeachments. When sitting for that Purpose, they shall be on Oath or Affirmation. When the President of the United States is tried, the Chief Justice shall preside: And no Person shall be convicted without the Concurrence of two thirds of the Members present.

Judgment in Cases of Impeachment shall not extend further than to removal from Office, and disqualification to hold and enjoy any Office of honor, Trust or Profit under the United States: but the Party convicted shall nevertheless be liable and subject to Indictment, Trial, Judgment and Punishment, according to Law.

Section. 4.

The Times, Places and Manner of holding Elections for Senators and Representatives, shall be prescribed in each State by the Legislature thereof; but the Congress may at any time by Law make or alter such Regulations, except as to the Places of chusing Senators.

The Congress shall assemble at least once in every Year, and such Meeting shall be on the first Monday in December, unless they shall by Law appoint a different Day.

Section. 5.

Each House shall be the Judge of the Elections, Returns and Qualifications of its own Members, and a Majority of each shall constitute a Quorum to do Business; but a smaller Number may adjourn from day to day, and may be authorized to compel the Attendance of absent Members, in such Manner, and under such Penalties as each House may provide.

Each House may determine the Rules of its Proceedings, punish its Members for disorderly Behaviour, and, with the Concurrence of two thirds, expel a Member.

Each House shall keep a Journal of its Proceedings, and from time to time publish the same, excepting such Parts as may in their

Judgment require Secrecy; and the Yeas and Nays of the Members of either House on any question shall, at the Desire of one fifth of those Present, be entered on the Journal.

Neither House, during the Session of Congress, shall, without the Consent of the other, adjourn for more than three days, nor to any other Place than that in which the two Houses shall be sitting.

Section. 6.

The Senators and Representatives shall receive a Compensation for their Services, to be ascertained by Law, and paid out of the Treasury of the United States. They shall in all Cases, except Treason, Felony and Breach of the Peace, be privileged from Arrest during their Attendance at the Session of their respective Houses, and in going to and returning from the same; and for any Speech or Debate in either House, they shall not be questioned in any other Place.

No Senator or Representative shall, during the Time for which he was elected, be appointed to any civil Office under the Authority of the United States, which shall have been created, or the Emoluments whereof shall have been encreased during such time; and no Person holding any Office under the United States, shall be a Member of either House during his Continuance in Office.

Section. 7.

All Bills for raising Revenue shall originate in the House of Representatives; but the Senate may propose or concur with Amendments as on other Bills.

Every Bill which shall have passed the House of Representatives and the Senate, shall, before it become a Law, be presented to the President of the United States; If he approve he shall sign it, but if not he shall return it, with his Objections to that House in which it shall have originated, who shall enter the Objections at large on their Journal, and proceed to reconsider it. If after such Reconsideration two thirds of that House shall agree to pass the Bill, it shall be sent, together with the Objections, to the other House, by which it shall likewise be reconsidered, and if approved by two thirds of that House, it shall become a Law. But in all such Cases the Votes of both Houses shall be determined by yeas and Nays, and the Names of the Persons voting for and against the Bill shall be entered on the

Journal of each House respectively. If any Bill shall not be returned by the President within ten Days (Sundays excepted) after it shall have been presented to him, the Same shall be a Law, in like Manner as if he had signed it, unless the Congress by their Adjournment prevent its Return, in which Case it shall not be a Law.

Every Order, Resolution, or Vote to which the Concurrence of the Senate and House of Representatives may be necessary (except on a question of Adjournment) shall be presented to the President of the United States; and before the Same shall take Effect, shall be approved by him, or being disapproved by him, shall be repassed by two thirds of the Senate and House of Representatives, according to the Rules and Limitations prescribed in the Case of a Bill.

Section. 8.

The Congress shall have Power To lay and collect Taxes, Duties, Imposts and Excises, to pay the Debts and provide for the common Defence and general Welfare of the United States; but all Duties, Imposts and Excises shall be uniform throughout the United States;

To borrow Money on the credit of the United States;

To regulate Commerce with foreign Nations, and among the several States, and with the Indian Tribes;

To establish an uniform Rule of Naturalization, and uniform Laws on the subject of Bankruptcies throughout the United States;

To coin Money, regulate the Value thereof, and of foreign Coin, and fix the Standard of Weights and Measures;

To provide for the Punishment of counterfeiting the Securities and current Coin of the United States;

To establish Post Offices and post Roads;

To promote the Progress of Science and useful Arts, by securing for limited Times to Authors and Inventors the exclusive Right to their respective Writings and Discoveries;

To constitute Tribunals inferior to the supreme Court;

To define and punish Piracies and Felonies committed on the high Seas, and Offences against the Law of Nations;

To declare War, grant Letters of Marque and Reprisal, and make Rules concerning Captures on Land and Water;

To raise and support Armies, but no Appropriation of Money to that Use shall be for a longer Term than two Years;

To provide and maintain a Navy; To make Rules for the Government and Regulation of the land and naval Forces;

To provide for calling forth the Militia to execute the Laws of the Union, suppress Insurrections and repel Invasions;

To provide for organizing, arming, and disciplining, the Militia, and for governing such Part of them as may be employed in the Service of the United States, reserving to the States respectively, the Appointment of the Officers, and the Authority of training the Militia according to the discipline prescribed by Congress;

To exercise exclusive Legislation in all Cases whatsoever, over such District (not exceeding ten Miles square) as may, by Cession of particular States, and the Acceptance of Congress, become the Seat of the Government of the United States, and to exercise like Authority over all Places purchased by the Consent of the Legislature of the State in which the Same shall be, for the Erection of Forts, Magazines, Arsenals, dock-Yards, and other needful Buildings;—And

To make all Laws which shall be necessary and proper for carrying into Execution the foregoing Powers, and all other Powers vested by this Constitution in the Government of the United States, or in any Department or Officer thereof.

Section. 9.

The Migration or Importation of such Persons as any of the States now existing shall think proper to admit, shall not be prohibited by the Congress prior to the Year one thousand eight hundred and eight, but a Tax or duty may be imposed on such Importation, not exceeding ten dollars for each Person.

The Privilege of the Writ of Habeas Corpus shall not be suspended, unless when in Cases of Rebellion or Invasion the public Safety may require it.

No Bill of Attainder or ex post facto Law shall be passed.

No Capitation, or other direct, Tax shall be laid, unless in Proportion to the Census or enumeration herein before directed to be taken.

No Tax or Duty shall be laid on Articles exported from any State.

No Preference shall be given by any Regulation of Commerce or Revenue to the Ports of one State over those of another: nor shall Vessels bound to, or from, one State, be obliged to enter, clear, or pay Duties in another.

No Money shall be drawn from the Treasury, but in Consequence of Appropriations made by Law; and a regular Statement and Account of the Receipts and Expenditures of all public Money shall be published from time to time.

No Title of Nobility shall be granted by the United States: And no Person holding any Office of Profit or Trust under them, shall, without the Consent of the Congress, accept of any present, Emolument, Office, or Title, of any kind whatever, from any King, Prince, or foreign State.

Section. 10.

No State shall enter into any Treaty, Alliance, or Confederation; grant Letters of Marque and Reprisal; coin Money; emit Bills of Credit; make any Thing but gold and silver Coin a Tender in Payment of Debts; pass any Bill of Attainder, ex post facto Law, or Law impairing the Obligation of Contracts, or grant any Title of Nobility.

No State shall, without the Consent of the Congress, lay any Imposts or Duties on Imports or Exports, except what may be absolutely necessary for executing it's inspection Laws: and the net Produce of all Duties and Imposts, laid by any State on Imports or Exports, shall be for the Use of the Treasury of the United States; and all such Laws shall be subject to the Revision and Controul of the Congress.

No State shall, without the Consent of Congress, lay any Duty of Tonnage, keep Troops, or Ships of War in time of Peace, enter into any Agreement or Compact with another State, or with a foreign Power, or engage in War, unless actually invaded, or in such imminent Danger as will not admit of delay.

Article. II.

Section. 1.

The executive Power shall be vested in a President of the United States of America. He shall hold his Office during the Term of four Years, and, together with the Vice President, chosen for the same Term, be elected, as follows

Each State shall appoint, in such Manner as the Legislature thereof may direct, a Number of Electors, equal to the whole Number of Senators and Representatives to which the State may be entitled in the Congress: but no Senator or Representative, or Person holding an Office of Trust or Profit under the United States, shall be appointed an Elector.

The Electors shall meet in their respective States, and vote by Ballot for two Persons, of whom one at least shall not be an Inhabitant of the same State with themselves. And they shall make a List of all the Persons voted for, and of the Number of Votes for each; which List they shall sign and certify, and transmit sealed to the Seat of the Government of the United States, directed to the President of the Senate. The President of the Senate shall, in the Presence of the Senate and House of Representatives, open all the Certificates, and the Votes shall then be counted. The Person having the greatest Number of Votes shall be the President, if such Number be a Majority of the whole Number of Electors appointed; and if there be more than one who have such Majority, and have an equal Number of Votes, then the House of Representatives shall immediately chuse by Ballot one of them for President; and if no Person have a Majority, then from the five highest on the List the said House shall in like Manner chuse the President. But in chusing the President, the Votes shall be taken by States, the Representation from each State having one Vote; A quorum for this Purpose shall consist of a Member or Members from two thirds of the States, and a Majority of all the States shall be necessary to a Choice. In every Case, after the Choice of the President, the Person having the greatest Number of Votes of the Electors shall be the Vice President. But if there should remain two or more who have equal Votes, the Senate shall chuse from them by Ballot the Vice President.

The Congress may determine the Time of chusing the Electors, and the Day on which they shall give their Votes; which Day shall be the same throughout the United States.

No Person except a natural born Citizen, or a Citizen of the United States, at the time of the Adoption of this Constitution, shall be eligible to the Office of President; neither shall any Person be eligible to that Office who shall not have attained to the Age of thirty five Years, and been fourteen Years a Resident within the United States.

In Case of the Removal of the President from Office, or of his Death, Resignation, or Inability to discharge the Powers and Duties of the said Office, the Same shall devolve on the Vice President, and the Congress may by Law provide for the Case of Removal, Death, Resignation or Inability, both of the President and Vice President, declaring what Officer shall then act as President, and such Officer shall act accordingly, until the Disability be removed, or a President shall be elected.

The President shall, at stated Times, receive for his Services, a Compensation, which shall neither be encreased nor diminished during the Period for which he shall have been elected, and he shall not receive within that Period any other Emolument from the United States, or any of them.

Before he enter on the Execution of his Office, he shall take the following Oath or Affirmation:—"I do solemnly swear (or affirm) that I will faithfully execute the Office of President of the United States, and will to the best of my Ability, preserve, protect and defend the Constitution of the United States."

Section. 2.

The President shall be Commander in Chief of the Army and Navy of the United States, and of the Militia of the several States, when called into the actual Service of the United States; he may require the Opinion, in writing, of the principal Officer in each of the executive Departments, upon any Subject relating to the Duties of their respective Offices, and he shall have Power to grant Reprieves and Pardons for Offences against the United States, except in Cases of Impeachment.

He shall have Power, by and with the Advice and Consent of the Senate, to make Treaties, provided two thirds of the Senators present concur; and he shall nominate, and by and with the Advice and Consent of the Senate, shall appoint Ambassadors, other public Ministers and Consuls, Judges of the supreme Court, and all other Officers of the United States, whose Appointments are not herein otherwise provided for, and which shall be established by Law: but the Congress may by Law vest the Appointment of such inferior Officers, as they think proper, in the President alone, in the Courts of Law, or in the Heads of Departments.

The President shall have Power to fill up all Vacancies that may happen during the Recess of the Senate, by granting Commissions which shall expire at the End of their next Session.

Section. 3.

He shall from time to time give to the Congress Information of the State of the Union, and recommend to their Consideration such Measures as he shall judge necessary and expedient; he may, on extraordinary Occasions, convene both Houses, or either of them, and in Case of Disagreement between them, with Respect to the Time of Adjournment, he may adjourn them to such Time as he shall think proper; he shall receive Ambassadors and other public Ministers; he shall take Care that the Laws be faithfully executed, and shall Commission all the Officers of the United States.

Section. 4.

The President, Vice President and all civil Officers of the United States, shall be removed from Office on Impeachment for, and Conviction of, Treason, Bribery, or other high Crimes and Misdemeanors.

Article III.

Section. 1.

The judicial Power of the United States, shall be vested in one supreme Court, and in such inferior Courts as the Congress may from time to time ordain and establish. The Judges, both of the supreme and inferior Courts, shall hold their Offices during good

Behaviour, and shall, at stated Times, receive for their Services, a Compensation, which shall not be diminished during their Continuance in Office.

Section. 2.

The judicial Power shall extend to all Cases, in Law and Equity, arising under this Constitution, the Laws of the United States, and Treaties made, or which shall be made, under their Authority;—to all Cases affecting Ambassadors, other public Ministers and Consuls;—to all Cases of admiralty and maritime Jurisdiction;—to Controversies to which the United States shall be a Party;—to Controversies between two or more States;— between a State and Citizens of another State,—between Citizens of different States,—between Citizens of the same State claiming Lands under Grants of different States, and between a State, or the Citizens thereof, and foreign States, Citizens or Subjects.

In all Cases affecting Ambassadors, other public Ministers and Consuls, and those in which a State shall be Party, the supreme Court shall have original Jurisdiction. In all the other Cases before mentioned, the supreme Court shall have appellate Jurisdiction, both as to Law and Fact, with such Exceptions, and under such Regulations as the Congress shall make.

The Trial of all Crimes, except in Cases of Impeachment, shall be by Jury; and such Trial shall be held in the State where the said Crimes shall have been committed; but when not committed within any State, the Trial shall be at such Place or Places as the Congress may by Law have directed.

Section. 3.

Treason against the United States, shall consist only in levying War against them, or in adhering to their Enemies, giving them Aid and Comfort. No Person shall be convicted of Treason unless on the Testimony of two Witnesses to the same overt Act, or on Confession in open Court.

The Congress shall have Power to declare the Punishment of Treason, but no Attainder of Treason shall work Corruption of Blood, or Forfeiture except during the Life of the Person attainted.

Article. IV.

Section. 1.

Full Faith and Credit shall be given in each State to the public Acts, Records, and judicial Proceedings of every other State. And the Congress may by general Laws prescribe the Manner in which such Acts, Records and Proceedings shall be proved, and the Effect thereof.

Section. 2.

The Citizens of each State shall be entitled to all Privileges and Immunities of Citizens in the several States.

A Person charged in any State with Treason, Felony, or other Crime, who shall flee from Justice, and be found in another State, shall on Demand of the executive Authority of the State from which he fled, be delivered up, to be removed to the State having Jurisdiction of the Crime.

No Person held to Service or Labour in one State, under the Laws thereof, escaping into another, shall, in Consequence of any Law or Regulation therein, be discharged from such Service or Labour, but shall be delivered up on Claim of the Party to whom such Service or Labour may be due.

Section. 3.

New States may be admitted by the Congress into this Union; but no new State shall be formed or erected within the Jurisdiction of any other State; nor any State be formed by the Junction of two or more States, or Parts of States, without the Consent of the Legislatures of the States concerned as well as of the Congress.

The Congress shall have Power to dispose of and make all needful Rules and Regulations respecting the Territory or other Property belonging to the United States; and nothing in this Constitution shall be so construed as to Prejudice any Claims of the United States, or of any particular State.

Section. 4.

The United States shall guarantee to every State in this Union a Republican Form of Government, and shall protect each of them against Invasion; and on Application of the Legislature, or of the Executive (when the Legislature cannot be convened), against domestic Violence.

Article. V.

The Congress, whenever two thirds of both Houses shall deem it necessary, shall propose Amendments to this Constitution, or, on the Application of the Legislatures of two thirds of the several States, shall call a Convention for proposing Amendments, which, in either Case, shall be valid to all Intents and Purposes, as Part of this Constitution, when ratified by the Legislatures of three fourths of the several States, or by Conventions in three fourths thereof, as the one or the other Mode of Ratification may be proposed by the Congress; Provided that no Amendment which may be made prior to the Year One thousand eight hundred and eight shall in any Manner affect the first and fourth Clauses in the Ninth Section of the first Article; and that no State, without its Consent, shall be deprived of its equal Suffrage in the Senate.

Article. VI.

All Debts contracted and Engagements entered into, before the Adoption of this Constitution, shall be as valid against the United States under this Constitution, as under the Confederation.

This Constitution, and the Laws of the United States which shall be made in Pursuance thereof; and all Treaties made, or which shall be made, under the Authority of the United States, shall be the supreme Law of the Land; and the Judges in every State shall be bound thereby, any Thing in the Constitution or Laws of any State to the Contrary notwithstanding.

The Senators and Representatives before mentioned, and the Members of the several State Legislatures, and all executive and judicial Officers, both of the United States and of the several States, shall be bound by Oath or Affirmation, to support this Constitution; but no religious Test shall ever be required as a Qualification to any Office or public Trust under the United States.

Article. VII.

The Ratification of the Conventions of nine States, shall be sufficient for the Establishment of this Constitution between the States so ratifying the Same.

The Word, "the," being interlined between the seventh and eighth Lines of the first Page, The Word "Thirty" being partly written on an Erazure in the fifteenth Line of the first Page, The Words "is tried" being interlined between the thirty second and thirty third Lines of the first Page and the Word "the" being interlined between the forty third and forty fourth Lines of the second Page.

Attest William Jackson Secretary

done in Convention by the Unanimous Consent of the States present the Seventeenth Day of September in the Year of our Lord one thousand seven hundred and Eighty seven and of the Independance of the United States of America the Twelfth In witness whereof We have hereunto subscribed our Names,

G°. Washington
Presidt and deputy from Virginia

Delaware

Geo: Read
Gunning Bedford jun
John Dickinson
Richard Bassett
Jaco: Broom

Maryland

James McHenry
Dan of St Thos. Jenifer
Danl. Carroll

Virginia

John Blair

James Madison Jr.

North Carolina

Wm. Blount
Richd. Dobbs Spaight
Hu Williamson

South Carolina

J. Rutledge
Charles Cotesworth Pinckney
Charles Pinckney
Pierce Butler

Georgia

William Few
Abr Baldwin

New Hampshire

John Langdon
Nicholas Gilman

Massachusetts

Nathaniel Gorham
Rufus King

Connecticut

Wm. Saml. Johnson
Roger Sherman

New York

Alexander Hamilton

New Jersey

Wil: Livingston
David Brearley
Wm. Paterson
Jona: Dayton

Pennsylvania

B Franklin
Thomas Mifflin
Robt. Morris
Geo. Clymer
Thos. FitzSimons
Jared Ingersoll
James Wilson
Gouv Morris.'"[186] (Emphasis added. Reformatted.)

The United States of America adopted the Bill of Rights on December 15, 1791.[187] A Library of Congress government website asks,

"Do you know your Bill of Rights? It is the first <u>10 amendments</u> to the U.S. Constitution, confirming the <u>fundamental rights</u> of American citizens."[188] (Emphasis added.)

Clearly, a large reason for the Bill of Rights was to restrict the Federal government from abusing its powers over the citizens.

From a National Archive government website, here is the preamble to the Bill of Rights,

"Congress of the United States
begun and held at the City of New-York, on
Wednesday the fourth of March, one thousand seven hundred and eighty nine.

THE Conventions of a number of the States, having at the time of their adopting the Constitution, expressed a desire, in order to prevent misconstruction or abuse of its powers, that further declaratory and restrictive clauses should be added: And as extending the ground of public confidence in the Government, will best ensure the beneficent ends of its institution.

RESOLVED by the Senate and House of Representatives of the United States of America, in Congress assembled, two thirds of both Houses concurring, that the following Articles be proposed to the Legislatures of the several States, as amendments to the Constitution of the United States, all, or any of which Articles, when ratified by three fourths of the said Legislatures, to be valid to all intents and purposes, as part of the said Constitution; viz.

ARTICLES in addition to, and Amendment of the Constitution of the United States of America, proposed by Congress, and ratified by the Legislatures of the several States, pursuant to the fifth Article of the original Constitution."[189] (Emphasis added.)

The U.S. Bill of Rights includes the following:

"Amendment I

Congress shall make no law respecting an establishment of religion, or prohibiting the free exercise thereof; or abridging the freedom of speech, or of the press; or the right of the people peaceably to assemble, and to petition the Government for a redress of grievances.

Amendment II

A well regulated Militia, being necessary to the security of a free State, the right of the people to keep and bear Arms, shall not be infringed.

Amendment III

No Soldier shall, in time of peace be quartered in any house, without the consent of the Owner, nor in time of war, but in a manner to be prescribed by law.

Amendment IV

The right of the people to be secure in their persons, houses, papers, and effects, against unreasonable searches and seizures, shall not be violated, and no Warrants shall issue, but upon probable cause, supported by Oath or affirmation, and particularly describing the place to be searched, and the persons or things to be seized.

Amendment V

No person shall be held to answer for a capital, or otherwise infamous crime, unless on a presentment or indictment of a Grand Jury, except in cases arising in the land or naval forces, or in the Militia, when in actual service in time of War or public danger; nor shall any person be subject for the same offence to be twice put in jeopardy of life or limb; nor shall be compelled in any criminal case to be a witness against himself, nor be deprived of life, liberty, or property, without due process of law; nor shall private property be taken for public use, without just compensation.

Amendment VI

In all criminal prosecutions, the accused shall enjoy the right to a speedy and public trial, by an impartial jury of the State and district wherein the crime shall have been committed, which district shall have been previously ascertained by law, and to be informed of the nature and cause of the accusation; to be confronted with the witnesses against him; to have compulsory process for obtaining witnesses in his favor, and to have the Assistance of Counsel for his defence.

Amendment VII

In Suits at common law, where the value in controversy shall exceed twenty dollars, the right of trial by jury shall be preserved, and no fact tried by a jury, shall be otherwise re-examined in any Court of the United States, than according to the rules of the common law.

Amendment VIII

Excessive bail shall not be required, nor excessive fines imposed, nor cruel and unusual punishments inflicted.

Amendment IX

The enumeration in the Constitution, of certain rights, shall not be construed to deny or disparage others retained by the people.

Amendment X

The powers not delegated to the United States by the Constitution, nor prohibited by it to the States, are reserved to the States respectively, or to the people."[190]

In addition, below are Constitutional Amendments 11-27 (with dates of these Amendments) found online in the U.S. National Archives website,

"AMENDMENT XI

Passed by Congress March 4, 1794. Ratified February 7, 1795.

Note: Article III, section 2, of the Constitution was modified by amendment 11. The Judicial power of the

United States shall not be construed to extend to any suit in law or equity, commenced or prosecuted against one of the United States by Citizens of another State, or by Citizens or Subjects of any Foreign State.

AMENDMENT XII

Passed by Congress December 9, 1803. Ratified June 15, 1804.

Note: A portion of Article II, section 1 of the Constitution was superseded by the 12th amendment. The Electors shall meet in their respective states and vote by ballot for President and Vice-President, one of whom, at least, shall not be an inhabitant of the same state with themselves; they shall name in their ballots the person voted for as President, and in distinct ballots the person voted for as Vice-President, and they shall make distinct lists of all persons voted for as President, and of all persons voted for as Vice-President, and of the number of votes for each, which lists they shall sign and certify, and transmit sealed to the seat of the government of the United States, directed to the President of the Senate; -- the President of the Senate shall, in the presence of the Senate and House of Representatives, open all the certificates and the votes shall then be counted; -- The person having the greatest number of votes for President, shall be the President, if such number be a majority of the whole number of Electors appointed; and if no person have such majority, then from the persons having the highest numbers not exceeding three on the list of those voted for as President, the House of Representatives shall choose immediately, by ballot, the President. But in choosing the President, the votes shall be taken by states, the representation from each state having one vote; a quorum for this purpose shall consist of a member or members from two-thirds of the states, and a majority of all the states shall be necessary to a choice. [And if the House of Representatives shall not choose a President whenever the right of choice shall devolve upon them, before the fourth day of March next following, then the

Vice-President shall act as President, as in case of the death or other constitutional disability of the President. --]* The person having the greatest number of votes as Vice-President, shall be the Vice-President, if such number be a majority of the whole number of Electors appointed, and if no person have a majority, then from the two highest numbers on the list, the Senate shall choose the Vice-President; a quorum for the purpose shall consist of two-thirds of the whole number of Senators, and a majority of the whole number shall be necessary to a choice. But no person constitutionally ineligible to the office of President shall be eligible to that of Vice-President of the United States.
*Superseded by section 3 of the 20th amendment.

AMENDMENT XIII

Passed by Congress January 31, 1865. Ratified December 6, 1865.

Note: A portion of Article IV, section 2, of the Constitution was superseded by the 13th amendment.

Section 1.

Neither slavery nor involuntary servitude, except as a punishment for crime whereof the party shall have been duly convicted, shall exist within the United States, or any place subject to their jurisdiction.

Section 2.

Congress shall have power to enforce this article by appropriate legislation.

AMENDMENT XIV

Passed by Congress June 13, 1866. Ratified July 9, 1868.

Note: Article I, section 2, of the Constitution was modified by section 2 of the 14th amendment.

Section 1.

All persons born or naturalized in the United States, and subject to the jurisdiction thereof, are citizens of the United States and of the State wherein they reside. No State shall make or enforce any law which shall abridge the privileges or immunities of citizens of the United States; nor shall any State deprive any person of life, liberty, or property, without due process of law; nor deny to any person within its jurisdiction the equal protection of the laws.

Section 2.

Representatives shall be apportioned among the several States according to their respective numbers, counting the whole number of persons in each State, excluding Indians not taxed. But when the right to vote at any election for the choice of electors for President and Vice-President of the United States, Representatives in Congress, the Executive and Judicial officers of a State, or the members of the Legislature thereof, is denied to any of the male inhabitants of such State, being twenty-one years of age,* and citizens of the United States, or in any way abridged, except for participation in rebellion, or other crime, the basis of representation therein shall be reduced in the proportion which the number of such male citizens shall bear to the whole number of male citizens twenty-one years of age in such State.

Section 3.

No person shall be a Senator or Representative in Congress, or elector of President and Vice-President, or hold any office, civil or military, under the United States, or under any State, who, having previously taken an oath, as a member of Congress, or as an officer of the United States, or as a member of any State legislature, or as an executive or judicial officer of any State, to support the Constitution of the United States, shall have engaged in insurrection or rebellion against the same, or given aid or comfort to the enemies thereof. But Congress may by a vote of two-thirds of each House, remove such disability.

Section 4.

The validity of the public debt of the United States, authorized by law, including debts incurred for payment of pensions and bounties for services in suppressing insurrection or rebellion, shall not be questioned. But neither the United States nor any State shall assume or pay any debt or obligation incurred in aid of insurrection or rebellion against the United States, or any claim for the loss or emancipation of any slave; but all such debts, obligations and claims shall be held illegal and void.

Section 5.

The Congress shall have the power to enforce, by appropriate legislation, the provisions of this article.

*Changed by section 1 of the 26th amendment.

AMENDMENT XV

Passed by Congress February 26, 1869. Ratified February 3, 1870.

Section 1.

The right of citizens of the United States to vote shall not be denied or abridged by the United States or by any State on account of race, color, or previous condition of servitude--

Section 2.

The Congress shall have the power to enforce this article by appropriate legislation.

AMENDMENT XVI

Passed by Congress July 2, 1909. Ratified February

3, 1913.

Note: Article I, section 9, of the Constitution was modified by amendment 16.

The Congress shall have power to lay and collect taxes on incomes, from whatever source derived, without apportionment among the several States, and without regard to any census or enumeration.

AMENDMENT XVII

Passed by Congress May 13, 1912. Ratified April 8, 1913.

Note: Article I, section 3, of the Constitution was modified by the 17th amendment.

The Senate of the United States shall be composed of two Senators from each State, elected by the people thereof, for six years; and each Senator shall have one vote. The electors in each State shall have the qualifications requisite for electors of the most numerous branch of the State legislatures.

When vacancies happen in the representation of any State in the Senate, the executive authority of such State shall issue writs of election to fill such vacancies: Provided, That the legislature of any State may empower the executive thereof to make temporary appointments until the people fill the vacancies by election as the legislature may direct.

This amendment shall not be so construed as to affect the election or term of any Senator chosen before it becomes valid as part of the Constitution.

AMENDMENT XVIII

Passed by Congress December 18, 1917. Ratified January 16, 1919. Repealed by amendment 21.

Section 1.

After one year from the ratification of this article the manufacture, sale, or transportation of intoxicating liquors within, the importation thereof into, or the exportation thereof from the United States and all territory subject to the jurisdiction thereof for beverage purposes is hereby prohibited.

Section 2.

The Congress and the several States shall have concurrent power to enforce this article by appropriate legislation.

Section 3.

This article shall be inoperative unless it shall have been ratified as an amendment to the Constitution by the legislatures of the several States, as provided in the Constitution, within seven years from the date of the submission hereof to the States by the Congress.

AMENDMENT XIX

Passed by Congress June 4, 1919. Ratified August 18, 1920.

The right of citizens of the United States to vote shall not be denied or abridged by the United States or by any State on account of sex.

Congress shall have power to enforce this article by appropriate legislation.

AMENDMENT XX

Passed by Congress March 2, 1932. Ratified January 23, 1933.

Note: Article I, section 4, of the Constitution was modified by section 2 of this amendment. In addition, a portion of the 12th amendment was superseded by section 3.

Section 1.

The terms of the President and the Vice President shall end at noon on the 20th day of January, and the terms of Senators and Representatives at noon on the 3d day of January, of the years in which such terms would have ended if this article had not been ratified; and the terms of their successors shall then begin.

Section 2.

The Congress shall assemble at least once in every year, and such meeting shall begin at noon on the 3d day of January, unless they shall by law appoint a different day.

Section 3.

If, at the time fixed for the beginning of the term of the President, the President elect shall have died, the Vice President elect shall become President. If a President shall not have been chosen before the time fixed for the beginning of his term, or if the President elect shall have failed to qualify, then the Vice President elect shall act as President until a President shall have qualified; and the Congress may by law provide for the case wherein neither a President elect nor a Vice President elect shall have qualified, declaring who shall then act as President, or the manner in which one who is to act shall be selected, and such person shall act accordingly until a President or Vice President shall have qualified.

Section 4.

The Congress may by law provide for the case of the death of any of the persons from whom the House of Representatives may choose a President whenever the right of choice shall have devolved upon them, and for the case of the death of any of the persons from whom the Senate may choose a Vice President whenever the right of choice shall have devolved upon them.

Section 5.

Sections 1 and 2 shall take effect on the 15th day of October following the ratification of this article.

Section 6.

This article shall be inoperative unless it shall have been ratified as an amendment to the Constitution by the legislatures of three-fourths of the several States within seven years from the date of its submission.

AMENDMENT XXI

Passed by Congress February 20, 1933. Ratified December 5, 1933.

Section 1.

The eighteenth article of amendment to the Constitution of the United States is hereby repealed.

Section 2.

The transportation or importation into any State, Territory, or possession of the United States for delivery or use therein of intoxicating liquors, in violation of the laws thereof, is hereby prohibited.

Section 3.

This article shall be inoperative unless it shall have been ratified as an amendment to the Constitution by conventions in the several States, as provided in the Constitution, within seven years from the date of the submission hereof to the States by the Congress.

AMENDMENT XXII

Passed by Congress March 21, 1947. Ratified February 27, 1951.

Section 1.

No person shall be elected to the office of the President more than twice, and no person who has held the office of President, or acted as President, for more than two years of a term to which some other person was elected President shall be elected to the office of the President more than once. But this Article shall not apply to any person holding the office of President when this Article was proposed by the Congress, and shall not prevent any person who may be holding the office of President, or acting as President, during the term within which this Article becomes operative from holding the office of President or acting as President during the remainder of such term.

Section 2.

This article shall be inoperative unless it shall have been ratified as an amendment to the Constitution by the legislatures of three-fourths of the several States within seven years from the date of its submission to the States by the Congress.

AMENDMENT XXIII

Passed by Congress June 16, 1960. Ratified March 29, 1961.

Section 1.

The District constituting the seat of Government of the United States shall appoint in such manner as the Congress may direct:

A number of electors of President and Vice President equal to the whole number of Senators and Representatives in Congress to which the District would be entitled if it were a State, but in no event more than the least populous State; they shall be in addition to those appointed by the States, but they shall be considered, for the purposes of the election of President and Vice President, to be electors appointed by a State; and they shall meet in the District and perform such duties as provided by the twelfth article of amendment.

Section 2.

The Congress shall have power to enforce this article by appropriate legislation.

AMENDMENT XXIV

Passed by Congress August 27, 1962. Ratified January 23, 1964.

Section 1.

The right of citizens of the United States to vote in any primary or other election for President or Vice President, for electors for President or Vice President, or for Senator or Representative in Congress, shall not be denied or abridged by the United States or any State by reason of failure to pay any poll tax or other tax.

Section 2.

The Congress shall have power to enforce this article by appropriate legislation.

AMENDMENT XXV

Passed by Congress July 6, 1965. Ratified February 10, 1967.

Note: Article II, section 1, of the Constitution was affected by the 25th amendment.

Section 1.

In case of the removal of the President from office or of his death or resignation, the Vice President shall become President.

Section 2.

Whenever there is a vacancy in the office of the Vice President, the President shall nominate a Vice President who shall take office upon confirmation by a majority vote of both Houses of Congress.

Section 3.

Whenever the President transmits to the President pro tempore of the Senate and the Speaker of the House of Representatives his written declaration that he is unable to discharge the powers and duties of his office, and until he transmits to them a written declaration to the contrary, such powers and duties shall be discharged by the Vice President as Acting President.

Section 4.

Whenever the Vice President and a majority of either the principal officers of the executive departments or of such other body as Congress may by law provide, transmit to the President pro tempore of the Senate and the Speaker of the House of Representatives their written declaration that the President is unable to discharge the powers and duties of his office, the Vice President shall immediately assume the powers and duties of the office as Acting President.

Thereafter, when the President transmits to the President pro tempore of the Senate and the Speaker of the House of Representatives his written declaration that no inability exists, he shall resume the powers and duties of his office unless the Vice President and a majority of either the principal officers of the executive department or of such other body as Congress may by law provide, transmit within four days to the President pro tempore of the Senate and the Speaker of the House of Representatives their written declaration that the President is unable to discharge the powers and duties of his office. Thereupon Congress shall decide the issue, assembling within forty-eight hours for that purpose if not in session. If the Congress, within twenty-one days after receipt of the latter written declaration, or, if Congress is not in session, within twenty-one days after Congress is required to assemble, determines by two-thirds vote of both Houses that the President is unable to discharge the powers and duties of his office, the Vice President shall continue to discharge the same as Acting President; otherwise, the President shall resume the powers and duties of his office.

AMENDMENT XXVI

Passed by Congress March 23, 1971. Ratified July 1, 1971.

Note: Amendment 14, section 2, of the Constitution was modified by section 1 of the 26th amendment.

Section 1.

The right of citizens of the United States, who are eighteen years of age or older, to vote shall not be denied or abridged by the United States or by any State on account of age.

Section 2.

The Congress shall have power to enforce this article by appropriate legislation.

AMENDMENT XXVII

Originally proposed Sept. 25, 1789. Ratified May 7, 1992.

No law, varying the compensation for the services of the Senators and Representatives, shall take effect, until an election of Representatives shall have intervened."[191] (Reformatted.)

ADDENDUM C

PRESIDENT GEORGE WASHINGTON'S FAREWELL ADDRESS (1796)

Here is an important transcript of **President George Washington's** *Farewell Address* (1796) found on ourdocuments.gov:

"Friends and Fellow Citizens:

The period for a new election of a citizen to administer the executive government of the United States being not far distant, and the time actually arrived when your thoughts must be employed in designating the person who is to be clothed with that important trust, it appears to me proper, especially as it may conduce to a more distinct expression of the public voice, that I should now apprise you of the resolution I have formed, to decline being considered among the number of those out of whom a choice is to be made.

I beg you, at the same time, to do me the justice to be assured that this resolution has not been taken without a strict regard to all the considerations appertaining to the relation which binds a dutiful citizen to his country; and that in withdrawing the tender of service, which silence in my situation might imply, I am influenced by no diminution of zeal for your future interest, no deficiency of grateful respect for your past kindness, but am supported by a full conviction that the step is compatible with both.

The acceptance of, and continuance hitherto in, the office to which your suffrages have twice called me have been a uniform sacrifice of inclination to the opinion of duty and to a deference for what appeared to be your desire. I constantly hoped that it would have been much earlier in my power, consistently with motives which I was not at liberty to disregard, to return to that retirement from which I had been reluctantly drawn. The strength of my inclination to do this, previous to the last election, had even led to the preparation of an address to declare it to you; but mature reflection on the then perplexed and critical posture of our affairs with foreign nations, and the unanimous advice of persons entitled to my confidence, impelled me to abandon the idea.

I rejoice that the state of your concerns, external as well as internal, no longer renders the pursuit of inclination incompatible with the sentiment of duty or propriety, and am persuaded, whatever partiality may be retained for my services, that, in the present circumstances of our country, you will not disapprove my determination to retire.

The impressions with which I first undertook the arduous trust were explained on the proper occasion. In the discharge of this trust, I will only say that I have, with good intentions, contributed towards the organization and administration of the government the best exertions of which a very fallible judgment was capable. Not unconscious in the outset of the inferiority of my qualifications, experience in my own eyes, perhaps still more in the eyes of others, has strengthened the motives to diffidence of myself; and every day the increasing weight of years admonishes me more and more that the shade of retirement is as necessary to me as it will be welcome. Satisfied that if any circumstances have given peculiar value to my services, they were temporary, I have the consolation to believe that, while choice and prudence invite me to quit the political scene, patriotism does not forbid it.

In looking forward to the moment which is intended to terminate the career of my public life, my feelings do not permit me to suspend the deep acknowledgment of that debt of gratitude which I owe to my beloved country for the many honors it has conferred upon me; still more for the steadfast confidence with which it has supported me; and for the opportunities I have thence enjoyed of manifesting my inviolable attachment, by services faithful and persevering, though in usefulness unequal to my zeal. If benefits have resulted to our country from these services, let it always be remembered to your praise, and as an instructive example in our annals, that under circumstances in which the passions, agitated in every direction, were liable to mislead, amidst appearances sometimes dubious, vicissitudes of fortune often discouraging, in situations in which not unfrequently want of success has countenanced the spirit of criticism, the constancy of your support was the essential prop of the efforts, and a guarantee of the plans by which they were effected. Profoundly penetrated with this idea, I shall carry it with me to my grave, as a strong incitement to unceasing vows that heaven may continue to you the choicest tokens of its beneficence; that your union and brotherly affection may be perpetual; that the free Constitution, which is the work of your hands, may be sacredly maintained; that its administration in every department may be stamped with wisdom and virtue; that, in fine, the happiness of the people of these States, under the auspices of liberty, may be made complete by so careful a preservation and so prudent a use of this blessing as will acquire to them the glory of recommending it to the applause, the affection, and adoption of every nation which is yet a stranger to it.

Here, perhaps, I ought to stop. But a solicitude for your welfare, which cannot end but with my life, and the apprehension of danger, natural to that solicitude, urge me, on an occasion like the present, to offer to your solemn contemplation, and to recommend to your frequent review, some sentiments which are the result of much reflection, of no inconsiderable observation, and which appear to me all-important to the permanency of your felicity as a people. These will be offered to you with the more freedom, as you can only see in them the disinterested warnings of a parting friend, who can possibly have no personal motive to bias his counsel. Nor can I forget, as an encouragement to it, your indulgent reception of my sentiments on a former and not dissimilar occasion.

Interwoven as is the love of liberty with every ligament of your hearts, no recommendation of mine is necessary to fortify or confirm the attachment.

The unity of government which constitutes you one people is also now dear to you. It is justly so, for it is a main pillar in the edifice of your real independence, the support of your tranquility at home, your peace abroad; of your safety; of your prosperity; of that very liberty which you so highly prize. But as it is easy to foresee that, from different causes and from different quarters, much pains will be taken, many artifices employed to weaken in your minds the conviction of this truth; as this is the point in your political fortress against which the batteries of internal and external enemies will be most constantly and actively (though often covertly and insidiously) directed, it is of infinite moment that you should properly estimate the immense value of your national union to your collective and individual happiness; that you should cherish a cordial, habitual, and immovable attachment to it; accustoming yourselves to think and speak of it as of the palladium of your political safety and prosperity; watching for its preservation with jealous anxiety; discountenancing whatever may suggest even a suspicion that it can in any event be abandoned; and indignantly frowning upon the first dawning of every attempt to alienate any portion of our country from the rest, or to enfeeble the sacred ties which now link together the various parts.

For this you have every inducement of sympathy and interest. Citizens, by birth or choice, of a common country, that country has a right to concentrate your affections. The name of American, which belongs to you in your national capacity, must always exalt the just pride of patriotism more than any appellation derived from local discriminations. With slight shades of difference, you have the same religion, manners, habits, and political principles. You have in a common cause fought and triumphed together; the independence and liberty you possess are the work of joint counsels, and joint efforts of common dangers, sufferings, and successes.

But these considerations, however powerfully they address themselves to your sensibility, are greatly outweighed by those which apply more immediately to your interest. Here every portion of our country finds the most commanding motives for carefully guarding and preserving the union of the whole.

The North, in an unrestrained intercourse with the South, protected by the equal laws of a common government, finds in the productions of the latter great additional resources of maritime and commercial enterprise and precious materials of manufacturing industry. The South, in the same intercourse, benefiting by the agency of the North, sees its agriculture grow and its commerce expand. Turning partly into its own channels the seamen of the North, it finds its particular navigation invigorated; and, while it contributes, in different ways, to nourish and increase the general mass of the national navigation, it looks forward to the protection of a maritime strength, to which itself is unequally adapted. The East, in a like intercourse with the West, already finds, and in the progressive improvement of interior communications by land and water, will more and more find a valuable vent for the commodities which it brings from abroad, or manufactures at home. The West derives from the East supplies requisite to its growth and comfort, and, what is perhaps of still greater consequence, it must of necessity owe the secure enjoyment of indispensable outlets for its own productions to the weight, influence, and the future maritime strength of the Atlantic side of the Union, directed by an indissoluble community of interest as one nation. Any other tenure by which the West can hold this essential advantage, whether derived from its own separate strength, or from an apostate and unnatural connection with any foreign power, must be intrinsically precarious.

While, then, every part of our country thus feels an immediate and particular interest in union, all the parts combined cannot fail to find in the united mass of means and efforts greater strength, greater resource, proportionably greater security from external danger, a less frequent interruption of their peace by foreign nations; and, what is of inestimable value, they must derive from union an exemption from those broils and wars between themselves, which so frequently afflict neighboring countries not tied together by the same governments, which their own rival ships alone would be sufficient to produce, but which opposite foreign alliances, attachments, and intrigues would stimulate and embitter. Hence, likewise, they will avoid the necessity of those overgrown military establishments which, under any form of government, are inauspicious to liberty, and which are to be regarded as particularly hostile to republican liberty. In this sense it is that your union ought to be considered as a main prop of your liberty, and that the love of the one ought to endear to you the preservation of the other.

These considerations speak a persuasive language to every reflecting and virtuous mind, and exhibit the continuance of the Union as a primary object of patriotic desire. Is there a doubt whether a common government can embrace so large a sphere? Let experience solve it. To listen to mere speculation in such a case were criminal. We are authorized to hope that a proper organization of the whole with the auxiliary agency of governments for the respective subdivisions, will afford a happy issue to the experiment. It is well worth a fair and full experiment. With such powerful and obvious motives to union, affecting all parts of our country, while experience shall not have demonstrated its impracticability, there will always be reason to distrust the patriotism of those who in any quarter may endeavor to weaken its bands.

In contemplating the causes which may disturb our Union, it occurs as matter of serious concern that any ground should have been furnished for characterizing parties by geographical discriminations, Northern and Southern, Atlantic and Western; whence designing men may endeavor to excite a belief that there is a real difference of local interests and views. One of the expedients of party to acquire influence within particular districts is to misrepresent the opinions and aims of other districts. You cannot shield yourselves too much against the jealousies and heartburnings which spring from these misrepresentations; they tend to render alien to each other those who ought to be bound together by fraternal affection. The inhabitants of our Western country have lately had a useful lesson on this head;

they have seen, in the negotiation by the Executive, and in the unanimous ratification by the Senate, of the treaty with Spain, and in the universal satisfaction at that event, throughout the United States, a decisive proof how unfounded were the suspicions propagated among them of a policy in the General Government and in the Atlantic States unfriendly to their interests in regard to the Mississippi; they have been witnesses to the formation of two treaties, that with Great Britain, and that with Spain, which secure to them everything they could desire, in respect to our foreign relations, towards confirming their prosperity. Will it not be their wisdom to rely for the preservation of these advantages on the Union by which they were procured? Will they not henceforth be deaf to those advisers, if such there are, who would sever them from their brethren and connect them with aliens?

To the efficacy and permanency of your Union, a government for the whole is indispensable. No alliance, however strict, between the parts can be an adequate substitute; they must inevitably experience the infractions and interruptions which all alliances in all times have experienced. Sensible of this momentous truth, you have improved upon your first essay, by the adoption of a constitution of government better calculated than your former for an intimate union, and for the efficacious management of your common concerns. This government, the offspring of our own choice, uninfluenced and unawed, adopted upon full investigation and mature deliberation, completely free in its principles, in the distribution of its powers, uniting security with energy, and containing within itself a provision for its own amendment, has a just claim to your confidence and your support. Respect for its authority, compliance with its laws, acquiescence in its measures, are duties enjoined by the fundamental maxims of true liberty. The basis of our political systems is the right of the people to make and to alter their constitutions of government. But the Constitution which at any time exists, till changed by an explicit and authentic act of the whole people, is sacredly obligatory upon all. The very idea of the power and the right of the people to establish government presupposes the duty of every individual to obey the established government.

All obstructions to the execution of the laws, all combinations and associations, under whatever plausible character, with the real design to direct, control, counteract, or awe the regular deliberation and action of the constituted authorities, are destructive of this fundamental principle, and of fatal tendency. They serve to organize faction, to give it an artificial and extraordinary force; to put, in the place of the delegated will of the nation the will of a party, often a small but artful and enterprising minority of the community; and, according to the alternate triumphs of different parties, to make the public administration the mirror of the ill-concerted and incongruous projects of faction, rather than the organ of consistent and wholesome plans digested by common counsels and modified by mutual interests.

However combinations or associations of the above description may now and then answer popular ends, they are likely, in the course of time and things, to become potent engines, by which cunning, ambitious, and unprincipled men will be enabled to subvert the power of the people and to usurp for themselves the reins of government, destroying afterwards the very engines which have lifted them to unjust dominion.

Towards the preservation of your government, and the permanency of your present happy state, it is requisite, not only that you steadily discountenance irregular oppositions to its acknowledged authority, but also that you resist with care the spirit of innovation upon its principles, however specious the pretexts. One method of assault may be to effect, in the forms of the Constitution, alterations which will impair the energy of the system, and thus to undermine what cannot be directly overthrown. In all the changes to which you may be invited, remember that time and habit are at least as necessary to fix the true character of governments as of other human institutions; that experience is the surest standard by which to test the real tendency of the existing constitution of a country; that facility in changes, upon the credit of mere hypothesis and opinion, exposes to perpetual change, from the endless variety of hypothesis and opinion; and remember, especially, that for the efficient management of your common interests, in a country so extensive as ours, a government of as much vigor as is consistent with the perfect security of liberty is indispensable. Liberty itself will find in such a government, with powers properly distributed and adjusted, its surest guardian. It is, indeed, little else than a name, where the government is too feeble to withstand the enterprises of faction, to confine each member of the society within the limits prescribed by the laws, and to maintain all in the secure and tranquil enjoyment of the rights of person and property.

I have already intimated to you the danger of parties in the State, with particular reference to the founding of them on geographical discriminations. Let me now take a more comprehensive view, and warn you in the most solemn manner against the baneful effects of the spirit of party generally.

This spirit, unfortunately, is inseparable from our nature, having its root in the strongest passions of the human mind. It exists under different shapes in all governments, more or less stifled, controlled, or repressed; but, in those of the popular form, it is seen in its greatest rankness, and is truly their worst enemy.

The alternate domination of one faction over another, sharpened by the spirit of revenge, natural to party dissension, which in different ages and countries has perpetrated the most horrid enormities, is itself a frightful despotism. But this leads at length to a more formal and permanent despotism. The disorders and miseries which result gradually incline the minds of men to seek security and repose in the absolute power of an individual; and sooner or later the chief of some prevailing faction, more able or more fortunate than his competitors, turns this disposition to the purposes of his own elevation, on the ruins of public liberty.

Without looking forward to an extremity of this kind (which nevertheless ought not to be entirely out of sight), the common and continual mischiefs of the spirit of party are sufficient to make it the interest and duty of a wise people to discourage and restrain it.

It serves always to distract the public councils and enfeeble the public administration. It agitates the community with ill-founded jealousies and false alarms, kindles the animosity of one part against another, foments occasionally riot and insurrection. It opens the door to foreign influence and corruption, which finds a facilitated access to the government itself through the channels of party passions. Thus the policy and the will of one country are subjected to the policy and will of another.

There is an opinion that parties in free countries are useful checks upon the administration of the government and serve to keep alive the spirit of liberty. This within certain limits is probably true; and in governments of a monarchical cast, patriotism may look with indulgence, if not with favor, upon the spirit of party. But in those of the popular character, in governments purely elective, it is a spirit not to be encouraged. From their natural tendency, it is certain there will always be enough of that spirit for every salutary purpose. And there being constant danger of excess, the effort ought to be by force of public opinion, to mitigate and assuage it. A fire not to be quenched, it demands a uniform vigilance to prevent its bursting into a flame, lest, instead of warming, it should consume.

It is important, likewise, that the habits of thinking in a free country should inspire caution in those entrusted with its administration, to confine themselves within their respective constitutional spheres, avoiding in the exercise of the powers of one department to encroach upon another. The spirit of encroachment tends to consolidate the powers of all the departments in one, and thus to create, whatever the form of government, a real despotism. A just estimate of that love of power, and proneness to abuse it, which predominates in the human heart, is sufficient to satisfy us of the truth of this position. The necessity of reciprocal checks in the exercise of political power, by dividing and distributing it into different depositaries, and constituting each the guardian of the public weal against invasions by the others, has been evinced by experiments ancient and modern; some of them in our country and under our own eyes. To preserve them must be as necessary as to institute them. If, in the opinion of the people, the distribution or modification of the constitutional powers be in any particular wrong, let it be corrected by an amendment in the way which the Constitution designates. But let there be no change by usurpation; for though this, in one instance, may be the instrument of good, it is the customary weapon by which free governments are destroyed. The precedent must always greatly overbalance in permanent evil any partial or transient benefit, which the use can at any time yield.

Of all the dispositions and habits which lead to political prosperity, religion and morality are indispensable supports. In vain would that man claim the tribute of patriotism, who should labor to subvert these great pillars of human happiness, these firmest props of the duties of men and citizens. The mere politician, equally with the pious man, ought to respect and to cherish them. A volume could not trace all their connections with private and public felicity. Let it simply be asked: Where is the security for property, for reputation, for life, if the sense of religious obligation desert the oaths which are the instruments of investigation in courts of justice? And let us with caution indulge the supposition that morality can be maintained without religion. Whatever may be conceded to the influence of refined education on minds of peculiar structure, reason and experience both forbid us to expect that national morality can prevail in exclusion of religious principle.

It is substantially true that virtue or morality is a necessary spring of popular government. The rule, indeed, extends with more or less force to every species of free government. Who that is a sincere friend to it can look with indifference upon attempts to shake the foundation of the fabric?

Promote then, as an object of primary importance, institutions for the general diffusion of knowledge. In proportion as the structure of a government gives force to public opinion, it is essential that public opinion should be enlightened.

As a very important source of strength and security, cherish public credit. One method of preserving it is to use it as sparingly as possible, avoiding occasions of expense by cultivating peace, but remembering also that timely disbursements to prepare for danger frequently prevent much greater disbursements to repel it, avoiding likewise the accumulation of debt, not only by shunning occasions of expense, but by vigorous exertion in time of peace to discharge the debts which unavoidable wars may have occasioned, not ungenerously throwing upon posterity the burden which we ourselves ought to bear. The execution of these maxims belongs to your representatives, but it is necessary that public opinion should co-operate. To facilitate to them the performance of their duty, it is essential that you should practically bear in mind that towards the payment of debts there must be revenue; that to have revenue there must be taxes; that no taxes can be devised which are not more or less inconvenient and unpleasant; that the intrinsic embarrassment, inseparable from the selection of the proper objects (which is always a choice of difficulties), ought to be a decisive motive for a candid construction of the conduct of the government in making it, and for a spirit of acquiescence in the measures for obtaining revenue, which the public exigencies may at any time dictate.

Observe good faith and justice towards all nations; cultivate peace and harmony with all. Religion and morality enjoin this conduct; and can it be, that good policy does not equally enjoin it? It will be worthy of a free, enlightened, and at no distant period, a great nation, to give to mankind the magnanimous and too novel example of a people always guided by an exalted justice and benevolence. Who can doubt that, in the course of time and things, the fruits of such a plan would richly repay any temporary advantages which might be lost by a steady adherence to it? Can it be that Providence has not connected the permanent felicity of a nation with its virtue? The experiment, at least, is recommended by every sentiment which ennobles human nature. Alas! is it rendered impossible by its vices?

In the execution of such a plan, nothing is more essential than that permanent, inveterate antipathies against particular nations, and passionate attachments for others, should be excluded; and that, in place of them, just and amicable feelings towards all should be cultivated. The nation which indulges towards another a habitual hatred or a habitual fondness is in some degree a slave. It is a slave to its animosity or to its affection, either of which is sufficient to lead it astray from its duty and its interest. Antipathy in one nation against another disposes each more readily to offer insult and injury, to lay hold of slight causes of umbrage, and to be haughty and intractable, when accidental or trifling occasions of dispute occur. Hence, frequent collisions, obstinate, envenomed, and bloody contests. The nation, prompted by ill-will and resentment, sometimes impels to war the government, contrary to the best calculations of policy. The government sometimes participates in the national propensity, and adopts through passion what reason would reject; at other times it makes the animosity of the nation subservient to projects of hostility instigated by pride, ambition, and other sinister and pernicious motives. The peace often, sometimes perhaps the liberty, of nations, has been the victim.

So likewise, a passionate attachment of one nation for another produces a variety of evils. Sympathy for the favorite nation, facilitating the illusion of an imaginary common interest in cases where no real common interest exists, and infusing into one the enmities of the other, betrays the former into a participation in the quarrels and wars of the latter without adequate inducement or justification. It leads also to concessions to the favorite nation of privileges denied to others which is apt doubly to injure the nation making the concessions; by unnecessarily parting with what ought to have been retained, and by exciting jealousy, ill-will, and a disposition to retaliate, in the parties from whom equal privileges are withheld. And it gives to ambitious, corrupted, or deluded citizens (who devote themselves to the favorite nation), facility to betray or sacrifice the interests of their own country, without odium, sometimes even with popularity; gilding, with the appearances of a virtuous sense of obligation, a commendable deference for public opinion, or a laudable zeal for public good, the base or foolish compliances of ambition, corruption, or infatuation.

As avenues to foreign influence in innumerable ways, such attachments are particularly alarming to the truly enlightened and independent patriot. How many opportunities do they afford to tamper with domestic factions, to practice the arts of seduction, to mislead public opinion, to influence or awe the public councils? Such an attachment of a small or weak towards a great and powerful nation dooms the former to be the satellite of the latter.

Against the insidious wiles of foreign influence (I conjure you to believe me, fellow-citizens) the jealousy of a free people ought to be constantly awake, since history and experience prove that foreign influence is one of the most baneful foes of republican government. But that jealousy to be useful must be impartial; else it becomes the instrument of the very influence to be avoided, instead of a defense against it. Excessive partiality for one foreign nation and excessive dislike of another cause those whom they actuate to see danger only on one side, and serve to veil and even second the arts of influence on the other. Real patriots who may resist the intrigues of the favorite are liable to become suspected and odious, while its tools and dupes usurp the applause and confidence of the people, to surrender their interests.

The great rule of conduct for us in regard to foreign nations is in extending our commercial relations, to have with them as little political connection as possible. So far as we have already formed engagements, let them be fulfilled with perfect good faith. Here let us stop. Europe has a set of primary interests which to us have none; or a very remote relation. Hence she must be engaged in frequent controversies, the causes of which are essentially foreign to our concerns. Hence, therefore, it must be unwise in us to implicate ourselves by artificial ties in the ordinary vicissitudes of her politics, or the ordinary combinations and collisions of her friendships or enmities.

Our detached and distant situation invites and enables us to pursue a different course. If we remain one people under an efficient government. the period is not far off when we may defy material injury from external annoyance; when we may take such an attitude as will cause the neutrality we may at any time resolve upon to be scrupulously respected; when belligerent nations, under the impossibility of making acquisitions upon us, will not lightly hazard the giving us provocation; when we may choose peace or war, as our interest, guided by justice, shall counsel.

Why forego the advantages of so peculiar a situation? Why quit our own to stand upon foreign ground? Why, by interweaving our destiny with that of any part of Europe, entangle our peace and prosperity in the toils of European ambition, rivalship, interest, humor or caprice?

It is our true policy to steer clear of permanent alliances with any portion of the foreign world; so far, I mean, as we are now at liberty to do it; for let me not be understood as capable of patronizing infidelity to existing engagements. I hold the maxim no less applicable to public than to private affairs, that honesty is always the best policy. I repeat it, therefore, let those engagements be observed in their genuine sense. But, in my opinion, it is unnecessary and would be unwise to extend them.

Taking care always to keep ourselves by suitable establishments on a respectable defensive posture, we may safely trust to temporary alliances for extraordinary emergencies.

Harmony, liberal intercourse with all nations, are recommended by policy, humanity, and interest. But even our commercial policy should hold an equal and impartial hand; neither seeking nor granting exclusive favors or preferences; consulting the natural course of things; diffusing and diversifying by gentle means the streams of commerce, but forcing nothing; establishing (with powers so disposed, in order to give trade a stable course, to define the rights of our merchants, and to enable the government to support them) conventional rules of intercourse, the best that present circumstances and mutual opinion will permit, but temporary, and liable to be from time to time abandoned or varied, as experience and circumstances shall dictate; constantly keeping in view that it is folly in one nation to look for disinterested favors from another; that it must pay with a portion of its independence for whatever it may accept under that character; that, by such acceptance, it may place itself in the condition of having given equivalents for nominal favors, and yet of being reproached with ingratitude for not giving more. There can be no greater error than to expect or calculate upon real favors from nation to nation. It is an illusion, which experience must cure, which a just pride ought to discard.

In offering to you, my countrymen, these counsels of an old and affectionate friend, I dare not hope they will make the strong and lasting impression I could wish; that they will control the usual current of the passions, or prevent our nation from running the course which has hitherto marked the destiny of nations. But, if I may even flatter myself that they may be productive of some partial benefit, some occasional good; that they may now and then recur to moderate the fury of party spirit, to warn against the mischiefs of foreign intrigue, to guard against the impostures of pretended patriotism; this hope will be a full recompense for the solicitude for your welfare, by which they have been dictated.

How far in the discharge of my official duties I have been guided by the principles which have been delineated, the public records and other evidences of my conduct must witness to you and to the world. To myself, the assurance of my own conscience is, that I have at least believed myself to be guided by them.

In relation to the still subsisting war in Europe, my proclamation of the twenty-second of April, 1793, is the index of my plan. Sanctioned by your approving voice, and by that of your representatives in both houses of Congress, the spirit of that measure has continually governed me, uninfluenced by any attempts to deter or divert me from it.

After deliberate examination, with the aid of the best lights I could obtain, I was well satisfied that our country, under all the circumstances of the case, had a right to take, and was bound in duty and interest to take, a neutral position. Having taken it, I determined, as far as should depend upon me, to maintain it, with moderation, perseverance, and firmness.

The considerations which respect the right to hold this conduct, it is not necessary on this occasion to detail. I will only observe that, according to my understanding of the matter, that right, so far from being denied by any of the belligerent powers, has been virtually admitted by all.

The duty of holding a neutral conduct may be inferred, without anything more, from the obligation which justice and humanity impose on every nation, in cases in which it is free to act, to maintain inviolate the relations of peace and amity towards other nations.

The inducements of interest for observing that conduct will best be referred to your own reflections and experience. With me a predominant motive has been to endeavor to gain time to our country to settle and mature its yet recent institutions, and to progress without interruption to that degree of strength and consistency which is necessary to give it, humanly speaking, the command of its own fortunes.

Though, in reviewing the incidents of my administration, I am unconscious of intentional error, I am nevertheless too sensible of my defects not to think it probable that I may have committed many errors. Whatever they may be, I fervently beseech the Almighty to avert or mitigate the evils to which they may tend. I shall also carry with me the hope that my country will never cease to view them with indulgence; and that, after forty five years of my life dedicated to its service with an upright zeal, the faults of incompetent abilities will be consigned to oblivion, as myself must soon be to the mansions of rest.

Relying on its kindness in this as in other things, and actuated by that fervent love towards it, which is so natural to a man who views in it the native soil of himself and his progenitors for several generations, I anticipate with pleasing expectation that retreat in which I promise myself to realize, without alloy, the sweet enjoyment of partaking, in the midst of my fellow-citizens, the benign influence of good laws under a free government, the ever-favorite object of my heart, and the happy reward, as I trust, of our mutual cares, labors, and dangers.

United States
19th September, 1796

Geo. Washington"[192]

(Reformatted.)

ADDENDUM D

PRESIDENT ABRAHAM LINCOLN'S GETTYSBURG ADDRESS

Here is an important document written by President Abraham Lincoln found on the website ourdocuments.gov:

"**Transcript of Gettysburg Address**

Executive Mansion,

Washington, , 186 .

Four score and seven years ago our fathers brought forth, upon this continent, a new nation, conceived in liberty, and dedicated to the proposition that "all men are created equal"

Now we are engaged in a great civil war, testing whether that nation, or any nation so conceived, and so dedicated, can long endure. We are met on a great battle field of that war. We have come to dedicate a portion of it, as a final resting place for those who died here, that the nation might live. This we may, in all propriety do. But, in a larger sense, we can not dedicate -- we can not consecrate -- we can not hallow, this ground-- The brave men, living and dead, who struggled here, have hallowed it, far above our poor power to add or detract. The world will little note, nor long remember what we say here; while it can never forget what they did here.

It is rather for us, the living, to stand here, we here be dedica-ted to the great task remaining before us -- that, from these honored dead we take increased devotion to that cause for which they here, gave the last full measure of devotion -- that we here highly resolve these dead shall not have died in vain; that the nation, shall have a new birth of freedom, and that government of the people by the people for the people, shall not perish from the earth."[193]

(Note: Typos and strike-outs are in the transcript. Also, reformatted.)

REFERENCES

[1]Santoso, A. (n.d.). 10 Richest People of All Time and How They Made Their Fortunes. Retrieved February 04, 2017, from http://www.neatorama.com/2008/07/09/10-richest-people-of-all-time-and-how-they-made-their-fortunes/#!qgEyq (Date of article: Wednesday, July 9, 2008)

[2]Santoso, A. (n.d.). 10 Richest People of All Time and How They Made Their Fortunes. Retrieved February 04, 2017, from http://www.neatorama.com/2008/07/09/10-richest-people-of-all-time-and-how-they-made-their-fortunes/#!qgEyq (Date of article: Wednesday, July 9, 2008)

[3]Kunzig, R. (2011, January). 7 Billion. *National Geographic, Special Series*, 40-41.

[4]Kunzig, R. (2011, January). 7 Billion. *National Geographic, Special Series*, 40-41.

[5]Kunzig, R. (2011, January). 7 Billion. *National Geographic, Special Series*, 40-41.

[6]U.S. and World Population Clock. (n.d.). Retrieved February 04, 2017, from http://www.census.gov/popclock/ (The U.S. Department of Commerce; U.S. Census Bureau)

[7]U.S. and World Population Clock. (n.d.). Retrieved May 15, 2014, from http://www.census.gov/popclock/ (The U.S. Department of Commerce; U.S. Census Bureau)

[8]U.S. and World Population Clock. (n.d.). Retrieved February 04, 2017, from http://www.census.gov/popclock/ (The U.S. Department of Commerce; U.S. Census Bureau)

[9]http://www.edd.ca.gov/Unemployment/Federal_Unemployment_Insurance_Extensions.htm (I retrieved the website information on a previous date; the earliest version of my book with this website citation is on or about 5-15-14). This information was no longer available on this specific website page by the State of California, California Employment Development Dept., when I returned as I was finishing my book on Feb. 4, 2017.)

[10]Alternative Measures of Labor Underutilization for States. (n.d.). Retrieved February 05, 2017, from https://www.bls.gov/lau/stalt.htm (U.S. Dept. of Labor; U.S. Bureau of Labor Statistics. Website states it was "Last Modified Date: January 27, 2017")

[11]Alternative Measures of Labor Underutilization for States. (n.d.). Retrieved February 05, 2017, from https://www.bls.gov/lau/stalt.htm (U.S. Dept. of Labor; U.S. Bureau of Labor Statistics. Website states

it was "Last Modified Date: January 27, 2017")

[12]Jacobson, L. (2015, January 23). PolitiFact: President's claim on unemployment rate is true, but has caveats. Retrieved February 05, 2017, from http://www.tampabay.com/news/business/politifact-presidents-claim-on-unemployment-rate-is-true-but-has-caveats/2214918 (Tampa Bay Times)

[13]Jacobson, L. (2015, January 23). PolitiFact: President's claim on unemployment rate is true, but has caveats. Retrieved February 05, 2017, from http://www.tampabay.com/news/business/politifact-presidents-claim-on-unemployment-rate-is-true-but-has-caveats/2214918 (Tampa Bay Times)

[14]Overview. (2016, February 02). Retrieved February 05, 2017, from http://thebulletin.org/overview (Bulletin of the Atomic Scientists.)

[15]Robert E. Lucas Jr. (n.d.). Retrieved February 16, 2017 from http://www.nobel-winners.com/Economics/robert_lucas.html

[16]Robert E. Lucas Jr.: The Concise Encyclopedia of Economics | Library of Economics and Liberty. (n.d.). Retrieved February 26, 2017 from http://www.econlib.org/library/Enc/bios/Lucas.html. (Note, online article citing Milton Friedman, "The Role of Monetary Policy," American Economic Review 58 (1968): 1–17; Edmund S. Phelps, "Money Wage Dynamics and Labor Market Equilibrium," Journal of Political Economy 76 (1968): 687–711. Bolded links with definitions/additional information in article omitted.)

[17]Hoover, K. D. (n.d.). Phillips Curve: The Concise Encyclopedia of Economics | Library of Economics and Liberty. Retrieved February 16, 2017 from http://www.econlib.org/library/Enc/PhillipsCurve.html (Author, Kevin D. Hoover) (Bolded links with definitions/additional information omitted.)

[18]Speech [by] Chairman Ben S. Bernanke At the Annual Meeting of the American Economic Association, Philadelphia, Pennsylvania January 3, 2014 The Federal Reserve: Looking Back, Looking Forward. (2014, January 3). Retrieved again February 05, 2017, from https://www.federalreserve.gov/newsevents/speech/bernanke20140103a.htm (Website last updated: January 3, 2014.) (Note: I previously retrieved this website.)

[19]Krugman, P. R. (1999, 2009). *The return of depression economics and the crisis of 2008* New York, N.Y., W. W. Norton & Company, Inc. (pp.9-10). (Note: Despite the title of this book, note that the epilogue in at least one version of the published book was written in

June 2009. Krugman wrote about a 1978 published article entitled *Monetary Theory and the Great Capitol Hill Baby-sitting Co-op Crisis*, by Joan and Richard Sweeney

[20]Krugman, P. R. (1999, 2009). *The return of depression economics and the crisis of 2008* New York, N.Y., W. W. Norton & Company, Inc. (p. 10). (Note: Despite the title of this book, note that the epilogue in at least one version of the published book was written in June 2009.)

[21]Krugman, P. R. (1999, 2009). *The return of depression economics and the crisis of 2008* New York, N.Y., W. W. Norton & Company, Inc. (p. 10). (Note: Despite the title of this book, note that the epilogue in at least one version of the published book was written in June 2009.)

[22]Krugman, P. R. (1999, 2009). *The return of depression economics and the crisis of 2008* New York, N.Y., W. W. Norton & Company, Inc. (p. 15). (Note: Despite the title of this book, note that the epilogue in at least one version of the published book was written in June 2009.)

[23] Krugman, P. R. (1999, 2009). *The return of depression economics and the crisis of 2008* New York, N.Y., W. W. Norton & Company, Inc. (p. 16). (Note: Despite the title of this book, note that the epilogue in at least one version of the published book was written in June 2009.)

[24]Krugman, P. R. (1999, 2009). *The return of depression economics and the crisis of 2008* New York, N.Y., W. W. Norton & Company, Inc. (pp. 16-20). (Note: Despite the title of this book, note that the epilogue in at least one version of the published book was written in June 2009.)

[25]Krugman, P. R. (1999, 2009). *The return of depression economics and the crisis of 2008* New York, N.Y., W. W. Norton & Company, Inc. (p. 20). (Note: Despite the title of this book, note that the epilogue in at least one version of the published book was written in June 2009.)

[26]Koesterich, R. (2011). *The ten trillion dollar gamble: The coming deficit debacle and how to invest now.* New York, N.Y., McGraw Hill. (p. xi.)

[27]Koesterich, R. (2011). *The ten trillion dollar gamble: The coming deficit debacle and how to invest now.* New York, N.Y., McGraw Hill. (p. xii.)

[28]Koesterich, R. (2011). *The ten trillion dollar gamble: The coming deficit debacle and how to invest now.* New York, N.Y., McGraw Hill. (p. 29.)

[29]Davidson, P. (2013, August 19). *Some furloughed federal workers may double dip.* Retrieved February 16, 2017 from http://www.usatoday.com/story/money/business/2013/10/19/federal-workers-shutdown-back-pay/3020525/

[30]Davidson, P. (2013, August 19). *Some furloughed federal workers may double dip.* Retrieved February 16, 2017 from http://www.usatoday.com/story/money/business/2013/10/19/federal-workers-shutdown-back-pay/3020525/

[31]Davidson, P. (2013, August 19). *Some furloughed federal workers may double dip.* Retrieved February 16, 2017 from http://www.usatoday.com/story/money/business/2013/10/19/federal-workers-shutdown-back-pay/3020525/

[32]U.S. Department of the Treasury, Bureau of the Fiscal Service. (n.d.). Debt to the Penny (Daily History Search Application). Retrieved February 17, 2017 from http://www.treasurydirect.gov/NP/debt/search?startMonth=01&startDay=01&startYear=2000&endMonth=&endDay=&endYear=
http://www.treasurydirect.gov/NP/debt/search?startMonth=01&startDay=01&startYear=2005&endMonth=&endDay=&endYear=
http://www.treasurydirect.gov/NP/debt/search?startMonth=01&startDay=01&startYear=2010&endMonth=&endDay=&endYear=   (Note: The amount as of 12-31-2009 was $12,311,349,677,512.03, and my graphs and table shows a $.03 difference of 12,311,349,677,512.00 (rounding error). Oh well, I guess my chart and graph were really not to the penny. But, I think this $.03 is an insignificant difference when dealing with trillions of dollars.)
http://www.treasurydirect.gov/NP/debt/search?startMonth=01&startDay=01&startYear=2015&endMonth=&endDay=&endYear=
(Total U.S. debt based on approx. Dec. 31, 1999, Dec. 31, 2004, Dec. 31, 2009, and Dec. 31, 2014, respectively.)

[33]U.S. Department of the Treasury, Bureau of the Fiscal Service. (n.d.). Debt to the Penny (Daily History Search Application). Retrieved February 17, 2017 from https://www.treasurydirect.gov/NP/debt/search?startMonth=01

[34]Central Bank Definition | Investopedia. (n.d.). Retrieved January 28, 2017 from http://www.investopedia.com/terms/c/centralbank.asp

[35]For the American Heritage Dictionary definition: central bank. (n.d.) *American Heritage® Dictionary of the English Language, Fifth Edition.* (2011). Retrieved December 17 2016 from http://www.thefreedictionary.com/central+bank

[36]FRB: Who owns the Federal Reserve? (n.d.). Retrieved January 28, 2015 from http://www.federalreserve.gov/faqs/about_14986.htm
(Website last updated: August 25, 2016
(Note: The website appears to have been changed while I was writing this book.)

[37] FRB: Who are the members of the Federal Reserve Board, and how are they selected? (n.d.). Retrieved February 19, 2017 from https://www.federalreserve.gov/faqs/about_12591.htm
(Website updated: January 11, 2017)

[38]FRB: Who owns the Federal Reserve? (n.d.). Retrieved January 28, 2015 from http://www.federalreserve.gov/faqs/about_14986.htm
(Website last updated: August 25, 2016 [Note: The website appears to have been changed while I was writing this book.)

[39]FRB: Who owns the Federal Reserve? (n.d.). Retrieved January 28, 2015 from http://www.federalreserve.gov/faqs/about_14986.htm
(Website last updated: August 25, 2016 Note: The website appears to have been changed while I was writing this book.)

[40]Who Owns the Federal Reserve Banks | In Plain English | St. Louis Fed. (n.d.). Retrieved October 18, 2016 from https://www.stlouisfed.org/in-plain-english/who-owns-the-federal-reserve-banks

[41]In Plain English - Making Sense of the Federal Reserve | St. Louis Fed. (n.d.). Retrieved January 22, 2017 from https://www.stlouisfed.org/in-plain-english (P. 5 of text version.)

[42]FRB: Press Release--Federal Reserve Board issues interim final rule regarding dividend payments on Reserve Bank capital stock-- February 18, 2016. (n.d.). Retrieved February 19, 2017 from https://www.federalreserve.gov/newsevents/press/bcreg/20160218a.htm

[43]From the Colonies to the 21st Century: The History of American Currency. (n.d.). Retrieved February 19, 2017 from www.uscurrency.gov/history

[44]From the Colonies to the 21st Century: The History of American

Currency. (n.d.). Retrieved February 19, 2017 from
www.uscurrency.gov/history

[45]From the Colonies to the 21st Century: The History of American Currency. (n.d.). Retrieved February 19, 2017 from www.uscurrency.gov/history

[46]From the Colonies to the 21st Century: The History of American Currency. (n.d.). Retrieved February 19, 2017 from www.uscurrency.gov/history

[47]Baack / Ohio State University, B. (n.d.). The Economics of the American Revolutionary War. Retrieved February 19, 2017 from http://eh.net/encyclopedia/the-economics-of-the-american-revolutionary-war/

[48]The United States Mint About Us. (n.d.). Retrieved January 28, 2017 from https://www.usmint.gov/about_the_mint/?cm_mmc=ExactTarget-_-Campaign-_-20150212+Kennedy+Rolls+and+Bags-_-Top+Nav+-+About&pf

[49]Bank of the United States - Facts & Summary - HISTORY.com. (n.d.). Retrieved January 28, 2017 from http://www.history.com/topics/bank-of-the-united-states

[50]Thomas Jefferson | whitehouse.gov. (n.d.). Retrieved February 19, 2017 from https://www.whitehouse.gov/1600/presidents/thomasjefferson

[51] Brown, E. H. (2007, 2008). *Web of debt: The shocking truth about our money system and how we can break free* Baton Rouge, LA, Third Millennium Press.

[52]Brown, E. H. (2007, 2008). *Web of debt: The shocking truth about our money system and how we can break free* Baton Rouge, LA, Third Millennium Press (p.78). (Emphasis added and other emphasis removed.) (Brown was quoting Jefferson's writing to Treasury Secretary Gallatin in 1815.)

[53]Bank of the United States - Facts & Summary - HISTORY.com. (n.d.). Retrieved January 28, 2017 from http://www.history.com/topics/bank-of-the-united-states

[54]Andrew Jackson | whitehouse.gov. (n.d.). Retrieved February 19, 2017 from https://www.whitehouse.gov/1600/presidents/andrewjackson

[55]Andrew Jackson | whitehouse.gov. (n.d.). Retrieved February 19, 2017 from https://www.whitehouse.gov/1600/presidents/andrewjackson

[56] Andrew Jackson | whitehouse.gov. (n.d.). Retrieved February 19, 2017 from
https://www.whitehouse.gov/1600/presidents/andrewjackson

[57] Andrew Jackson | whitehouse.gov. (n.d.). Retrieved February 19, 2017 from
https://www.whitehouse.gov/1600/presidents/andrewjackson

[58] Brown, E. H. (2007, 2008). *Web of debt: The shocking truth about our money system and how we can break free* Baton Rouge, LA, Third Millennium Press (p.81). (Brown quoting President Andrew Jackson.)

[59] Brown, E. H. (2007, 2008). *Web of debt: The shocking truth about our money system and how we can break free* Baton Rouge, LA, Third Millennium Press (p.80).

[60] Brown, E. H. (2007, 2008). *Web of debt: The shocking truth about our money system and how we can break free* Baton Rouge, LA, Third Millennium Press (p.80).

[61] Andrew Jackson | whitehouse.gov. (n.d.). Retrieved February 19, 2017 from
https://www.whitehouse.gov/1600/presidents/andrewjackson

[62] Bank of the United States - Facts & Summary - HISTORY.com. (n.d.). Retrieved January 28, 2017 from
http://www.history.com/topics/bank-of-the-united-states

[63] Andrew Jackson narrowly escapes assassination - Jan 30, 1835 - HISTORY.com. (n.d.). Retrieved February 19, 2017 from
http://www.history.com/this-day-in-history/andrew-jackson-narrowly-escapes-assassination

[64] Andrew Jackson narrowly escapes assassination - Jan 30, 1835 - HISTORY.com. (n.d.). Retrieved February 19, 2017 from
http://www.history.com/this-day-in-history/andrew-jackson-narrowly-escapes-assassination

[65] Andrew Jackson narrowly escapes assassination - Jan 30, 1835 - HISTORY.com. (n.d.). Retrieved February 19, 2017 from
http://www.history.com/this-day-in-history/andrew-jackson-narrowly-escapes-assassination

[66] Andrew Jackson narrowly escapes assassination - Jan 30, 1835 - HISTORY.com. (n.d.). Retrieved February 19, 2017 from
http://www.history.com/this-day-in-history/andrew-jackson-narrowly-escapes-assassination

[67] Brown, E. H. (2007, 2008). *Web of debt: The shocking truth about*

our money system and how we can break free Baton Rouge, LA, Third Millennium Press (p.82). (Note: Brown footnoted that President Bill Clinton had balanced the budget, but had not reduced the huge $5 trillion of national debt in 2000. I note that there is a big difference between balancing the annual national budget and reducing the cumulative national debt to zero.)

[68]Brown, E. H. (2007, 2008). *Web of debt: The shocking truth about our money system and how we can break free* Baton Rouge, LA, Third Millennium Press (p.83).

[69]Abraham Lincoln | whitehouse.gov. (n.d.). Retrieved from February 19, 2017 https://www.whitehouse.gov/1600/presidents/abrahamlincoln

[70]Brown, E. H. (2007, 2008). *Web of debt: The shocking truth about our money system and how we can break free* Baton Rouge, LA, Third Millennium Press (p.83).

[71]Lincoln, A. (n.d.). Transcript of Gettysburg Address (1863) (print-friendly version). Retrieved February 26, 2017 from https://www.ourdocuments.gov/print_friendly.php?flash=true&page=transcript&doc=36&title=Transcript+of+Gettysburg+Address+ (1863) (Note: Website states, "Abraham Lincoln, Draft of the Gettysburg Address: Nicolay Copy. Transcribed and annotated by the Lincoln Studies Center, Knox College, Galesburg, Illinois. Available at Abraham Lincoln Papers at the Library of Congress, Manuscript Division (Washington, D.C.: American Memory Project, [2000-02]),") (Also note: Typos and strike-outs are in the transcript. Reformatted.)

[72]Brown, E. H. (2007, 2008). *Web of debt: The shocking truth about our money system and how we can break free* Baton Rouge, LA, Third Millennium Press (p.84).

[73]Brown, E. H. (2007, 2008). *Web of debt: The shocking truth about our money system and how we can break free* Baton Rouge, LA, Third Millennium Press (p.84).

[74]Brown, E. H. (2007, 2008). *Web of debt: The shocking truth about our money system and how we can break free* Baton Rouge, LA, Third Millennium Press (p.84-85).

[75]Fiat Money | Definition of Fiat Money by Merriam-Webster. (n.d.). Retrieved February 19, 2017 from http://www.merriam-webster.com/dictionary/fiat%20money

[76]1800-1899. (n.d.). Retrieved February 19, 2017 from https://www.treasury.gov/about/history/Pages/1800-1899.aspx

(Website last updated on Last Updated: 10/2/2010 5:10 PM)

[77]Brown, E. H. (2007, 2008). *Web of debt: The shocking truth about our money system and how we can break free* Baton Rouge, LA, Third Millennium Press (p. xii).

[78]1800-1899. (n.d.). Retrieved February 19, 2017 from https://www.treasury.gov/about/history/Pages/1800-1899.aspx
(Website last updated on Last Updated: 10/2/2010 5:10 PM)

[79]1800-1899. (n.d.). Retrieved February 19, 2017 from https://www.treasury.gov/about/history/Pages/1800-1899.aspx
(Website last updated on Last Updated: 10/2/2010 5:10 PM)

[80]1900-Present. (n.d.). Retrieved February 26, 2017 from https://www.treasury.gov/about/history/Pages/1900-Present.aspx
(Website last updated on Last Updated: 3/30/2012 5:21 PM)

[81]Woodrow Wilson Quote - Liberty Quotes Blog. (n.d.). Retrieved February 19, 2017 from http://quotes.liberty-tree.ca/quote_blog/Woodrow.Wilson.Quote.51CE
(Website states on top, "Questionable Woodrow Wilson Quote.")
(Website citing Source of "Attributed. In reference to signing the Federal Reserve Act in 1913. Most likely a compilation of 2 quotes from his book *The New Freedom*, 1916. No source found for 'I am a most unhappy man. I have unwittingly ruined my country.'")

[82]FRB: Is the Federal Reserve Act going to expire? (n.d.). Retrieved February 19, 2017 from http://www.federalreserve.gov/faqs/is-the-federal-reserve-act-going-to-expire.htm
(Website last updated: April 22, 2016.)

[83]John F. Kennedy | whitehouse.gov. (n.d.). Retrieved December 6, 2016 from https://www.whitehouse.gov/1600/presidents/johnfkennedy

[84]Kennedy, J. F., Kennedy, C., & Kennedy, R. F. (2016). Introduction. In *Profiles in courage* (p. xii). NY: Harper Perennial. (Page xiii of Introduction written by Caroline Kennedy. Introduction dated in book and copyright 2003. Foreword written by Robert F. Kennedy, dated in book December 18, 1963 (copyright 1964). Book was originally published by Harper & Brothers in 1956. Harper Perennial - First Olive edition of book published 2016.)

[85] John F. Kennedy | whitehouse.gov. (n.d.). Retrieved December 6, 2016 from https://www.whitehouse.gov/1600/presidents/johnfkennedy

[86]John F. Kennedy | whitehouse.gov. (n.d.). Retrieved December 6,

2016 from
https://www.whitehouse.gov/1600/presidents/johnfkennedy

[87] John F. Kennedy | whitehouse.gov. (n.d.). Retrieved December 6, 2016 from
https://www.whitehouse.gov/1600/presidents/johnfkennedy

[88] Listed Citation: "John F. Kennedy: "Executive Order 11110—Amendment of Executive Order No. 10289 as Amended, Relating to the Performance of Certain Functions Affecting the Department of the Treasury," June 4, 1963. (Note. Website states, "© 1999-2017 - Gerhard Peters and John T. Woolley - The American Presidency Project."

[89] John F. Kennedy | whitehouse.gov. (n.d.). Retrieved December 6, 2016 from
https://www.whitehouse.gov/1600/presidents/johnfkennedy

[90] About (Silver Certificates). (n.d.). Retrieved February 15, 2017, from
https://www.treasury.gov/about/history/collections/Pages/silver.aspx
(Website states that it was, "Last Updated: December 12, 2008 Silver Certificates.")

[91] U.S. Bureau of Engraving and Printing - U.S. Currency. (n.d.). Retrieved Jan. 28, 2017 from
http://www.moneyfactory.gov/uscurrency.html

[92] Brown, E. H. (2007, 2008). *Web of debt: The shocking truth about our money system and how we can break free* Baton Rouge, LA, Third Millennium Press (p.2).

[93] Biography.com Editors. (n.d.). Ron Paul Biography. Retrieved February 26, 2017 from http://www.biography.com/people/ron-paul-265881 (Note: Publisher is A&E Television Networks; Last updated: April 20, 2015.)

[94] Paul, R. (2009). *End the Fed*. New York, NY: Grand Central Publishing (a division of Hachette Book Group, Inc.). (Copyright by The Foundation for Rational Economics and Education, Inc.)

[95] Paul, R. (2009). End the Fed. New York, NY: Grand Central Publishing (a division of Hachette Book Group, Inc.) (pp. 183-84). (Copyright by The Foundation for Rational Economics and Education, Inc.)

[96] Brown, E. H. (2007, 2008). *Web of debt: The shocking truth about our money system and how we can break free* Baton Rouge, LA, Third Millennium Press (p.ix).

[97]Paul, R. (2009). *End the Fed*. New York, NY: Grand Central Publishing (a division of Hachette Book Group, Inc.) (pp. 207-08). (Copyright by The Foundation for Rational Economics and Education, Inc.)

[98] Paul, R. (2009). *End the Fed*. New York, NY: Grand Central Publishing (a division of Hachette Book Group, Inc.) (pp. 159-60). (Copyright by The Foundation for Rational Economics and Education, Inc.)

[99]Paul, R. (2009). *End the Fed*. New York, NY: Grand Central Publishing (a division of Hachette Book Group, Inc.) (p. 140). (Copyright by The Foundation for Rational Economics and Education, Inc.)

[100]Paul, R. (2009). *End the Fed*. New York, NY: Grand Central Publishing (a division of Hachette Book Group, Inc.) (p. 150). (Copyright by The Foundation for Rational Economics and Education, Inc.)

[101] Paul, R. (2009). End the Fed. New York, NY: Grand Central Publishing (a division of Hachette Book Group, Inc.) (p. 142). (Copyright by The Foundation for Rational Economics and Education, Inc.)

[102]Oligarchy | Define Oligarchy at Dictionary.com. (n.d.). Retrieved February 26, 2017 from http://www.dictionary.com/browse/oligarchy (The American Heritage® New Dictionary of Cultural Literacy, Third Edition Copyright © 2005 by Houghton Mifflin Company. Published by Houghton Mifflin Company. All rights reserved.)

[103] Jimmy Carter: America Is Not A Democracy Anymore (AUDIO). (n.d.). Retrieved December 27, 2016 from http://talkingpointsmemo.com/livewire/jimmy-carter-us-oligarchy-bribes (Note: [with audio] By Sara Jerde; Published July 31, 2015).

[104]Jimmy Carter: America Is Not A Democracy Anymore (AUDIO). (n.d.). Retrieved December 27, 2016 from http://talkingpointsmemo.com/livewire/jimmy-carter-us-oligarchy-bribes (Note: [with audio] By Sara Jerde; Published July 31, 2015)

[105]Jimmy Carter: America Is Not A Democracy Anymore (AUDIO). (n.d.). Retrieved December 27, 2016 from http://talkingpointsmemo.com/livewire/jimmy-carter-us-oligarchy-bribes Note: [with audio] By Sara Jerde; Published July 31, 2015)

[106]Federal Citizen Information Center: Our Flag. (n.d.). Retrieved February 07, 2017, from https://publications.usa.gov/epublications/ourflag/pledge.htm

[107]Paul, R. (2009). *End the Fed*. New York, NY: Grand Central Publishing (a division of Hachette Book Group, Inc.) (p. 180). (Copyright by The Foundation for Rational Economics and Education, Inc.)

[108] Paul, R. (2009). *End the Fed*. New York, NY: Grand Central Publishing (a division of Hachette Book Group, Inc.) (pp. 203-04). (Copyright by The Foundation for Rational Economics and Education, Inc.)

[109]Forbes, S., & Ames, E. (2014). Money. How the destruction of the dollar threatens the global economy - and what we can do about it. 2014, New York, N.Y., McGraw Hill Education.

[110]Forbes, S., & Ames, E. (2014). Money: How the destruction of the dollar threatens the global economy - and what we can do about it. 2014, New York, N.Y., McGraw Hill Education (In front In Remembrance page.)

[111]1 Timothy 6:10 KJV - Bible Gateway. (n.d.). Retrieved February 26, 2017 from https://www.biblegateway.com/passage/?search=1+Timothy+6%3A10&version=KJV
(Note: Website includes the words "King James Version (KJV) Public Domain.")

[112]Forbes, S., & Ames, E. (2014). *Money: How the destruction of the dollar threatens the global economy - and what we can do about it.* 2014, New York, N.Y., McGraw Hill Education (p. 152).

[113]Forbes, S., & Ames, E. (2014). Money: How the destruction of the dollar threatens the global economy - and what we can do about it. 2014, New York, N.Y., McGraw Hill Education (p. 155).

[114]Paul, R. (2009). *End the Fed*. New York, NY: Grand Central Publishing (a division of Hachette Book Group, Inc.) (p. 187). (Copyright by The Foundation for Rational Economics and Education, Inc.)

[115]Paul, R. (2009). End the Fed. New York, NY: Grand Central Publishing (a division of Hachette Book Group, Inc.) (p. 205). (Copyright by The Foundation for Rational Economics and Education, Inc.)

[116]Brown, E. H. (2007, 2008). *Web of debt: The shocking truth about our money system and how we can break free* Baton Rouge, LA, Third Millennium Press (p.20).

[117] *Declaration of Independence*: A Transcription | National Archives. (n.d.). Retrieved February 26, 2017

https://www.archives.gov/founding-docs/declaration-transcript

[118]The Constitution of the United States: A Transcription | National Archives. (n.d.). Retrieved January 11, 2017 from https://www.archives.gov/founding-docs/constitution-transcript

[119]About the Federalist Papers - Congress.gov Resources. (n.d.). Retrieved February 26, 2017 from https://www.congress.gov/resources/display/content/About+the+Federalist+Papers (Note: Regarding the authors, the website generally explains, "The Federalist, commonly referred to as the Federalist Papers, is a series of 85 essays written by Alexander Hamilton, John Jay, and James Madison between October 1787 and May 1788. The essays were published anonymously, under the pen name 'Publius,' in various New York state newspapers of the time.").

[120]The Federalist Papers - Congress.gov Resources -. (n.d.). Retrieved February 26, 2017 from https://www.congress.gov/resources/display/content/The+Federalist+Papers (Note: Regarding the authors, the website generally explains, "The Federalist, commonly referred to as the Federalist Papers, is a series of 85 essays written by Alexander Hamilton, John Jay, and James Madison between October 1787 and May 1788. The essays were published anonymously, under the pen name 'Publius,' in various New York state newspapers of the time.").

[121]The Constitution of the United States: A Transcription | National Archives. (n.d.). Retrieved January 11, 2017 from https://www.archives.gov/founding-docs/constitution-transcript

[122]Legislative Department, Article 1. (2016). *In The Constitution of the United States of America: Analysis and interpretation; Centennial edition, Interim edition: Analysis of cases decided by the Supreme Court of the United States to June 27, 2016* (p. 324). Washington, DC: U.S. GOVERNMENT PUBLISHING OFFICE. ((Note: This material found in the U.S. Cong. (2016). THE CONSTITUTION of the UNITED STATES OF AMERICA ANALYSIS AND INTERPRETATION Centennial Edition INTERIM EDITION: ANALYSIS OF CASES DECIDED BY THE SUPREME COURT OF THE UNITED STATES TO JUNE 27, 2016 (p. 324) [Cong. Doc. 112-9 from 112th Cong., 2nd sess.]. Washington, DC: U.S. GOVERNMENT PUBLISHING OFFICE. PREPARED BY THE CONGRESSIONAL RESEARCH SERVICE LIBRARY OF CONGRESS (Website Retrieved and PDF downloaded on 12-26-16 at https://www.congress.gov/constitution-annotated) MICHAEL J. GARCIA, KATE M. MANUEL, AND ANDREW NOLAN, ATTORNEY

EDITORS, MEGHAN TOTTEN, LEGAL EDITOR (Quotation in my book is citing 1464 McCulloch v. Maryland, 17 U.S. (4 Wheat.) 316 (1819). 1465 Veazie Bank v. Fenno, 75 U.S. (8 Wall.) 533 (1869). 1466 75 U.S. at 548. 1467 National Bank v. United States, 101 U.S. 1 (1880). 1468 Nortz v. United States, 249 U.S. 317 (1935). 1469 Legal Tender Cases (Knox v. Lee), 79 U.S. (12 Wall.) 457, 549 (1871); Juilliard v. Greenman, 110 U.S. 421, 449 (1884). 1470 Legal Tender Cases (Knox v. Lee), 79 U.S. (12 Wall.) 457 (1871). 1471 Norman v. Baltimore & Ohio R.R., 294 U.S. 240 (1935). 1472 Ling Su Fan v. United States, 218 U.S. 302 (1910).))

[123]Brown, E. H. (2007, 2008). Web of debt: The shocking truth about our money system and how we can break free Baton Rouge, LA, Third Millennium Press (p.21).

[124]Brown, E. H. (2007, 2008). *Web of debt: The shocking truth about our money system and how we can break free* Baton Rouge, LA, Third Millennium Press (p.3).

[125]Brown, E. H. (2007, 2008). *Web of debt: The shocking truth about our money system and how we can break free* Baton Rouge, LA, Third Millennium Press (p.6).

[126]Brown, E. H. (2007, 2008). *Web of debt: The shocking truth about our money system and how we can break free* Baton Rouge, LA, Third Millennium Press (p.6).

[127]FRB: Who owns the Federal Reserve? (n.d.). Retrieved 1-28-15 from http://www.federalreserve.gov/faqs/about_14986.htm (Website last updated: August 25, 2016)

[128]FRB: Oversight of the Federal Reserve System - Credit and Liquidity Programs and the Balance Sheet. (n.d.). Retrieved February 26, 2017 from https://www.federalreserve.gov/monetarypolicy/bst_oversight.htm (Website page states it was last updated: "April 24, 2009")

[129]The Fed Audit - Senator Bernie Sanders of Vermont. (n.d.). Retrieved January 28, 2017 from http://www.sanders.senate.gov/newsroom/press-releases/the-fed-audit (Note: A United States Government Accountability Office (GAO) report is also downloadable from this website.)

[130]Paul, R. (2009). *End the Fed*. New York, NY: Grand Central Publishing (a division of Hachette Book Group, Inc.) (p. 198). (Copyright by The Foundation for Rational Economics and Education, Inc.)

[131]Gillespie, P. (2016, September 27). *Donald Trump claims Fed is*

'more political' than Clinton - Sep. 27, 2016. Retrieved March 1, 2017 from http://money.cnn.com/2016/09/27/investing/debate-trump-federal-reserve-janet-yellen/ (Note: Website also states, "CNNMoney's Heather Long contributed to this report." In addition, article's website embedded internet links for words "central argument" is linked to http://money.cnn.com/2016/09/06/investing/donald-trump-fed-false-economy/?iid=EL and "'ashamed of herself'" is linked to http://money.cnn.com/2016/09/13/investing/stocks-donald-trump-janet-yellen-federal-reserve/?iid=EL.)

[132]Investment Bank - IB Definition | Investopedia. (n.d.). Retrieved February 26, 2017 from http://www.investopedia.com/terms/i/investmentbank.asp

[133] Rickards, J. (2012, August 27). *Repeal of Glass-Steagall caused the financial crisis, The repeal of the law separating commercial and investment banking caused the 2008 financial crisis.* Retrieved February 26, 2017 from http://www.usnews.com/opinion/blogs/economic-intelligence/2012/08/27/repeal-of-glass-steagall-caused-the-financial-crisis

[134]Ritholtz, B. (2012, August 4). Repeal of Glass-Steagall: Not a cause, but a multiplier - The Washington Post. Retrieved February 26, 2017 from http://www.washingtonpost.com/repeal-of-glass-steagall-not-a-cause-but-a-multiplier/2012/08/02/gJQAuvvRXX_story.html

[135]Ritholtz, B. (2012, August 4). *Repeal of Glass-Steagall: Not a cause, but a multiplier* - The Washington Post. Retrieved February 26, 2017 from http://www.washingtonpost.com/repeal-of-glass-steagall-not-a-cause-but-a-multiplier/2012/08/02/gJQAuvvRXX_story.html

[136]Ritholtz, B. (2012, August 4). Repeal of Glass-Steagall: Not a cause, but a multiplier - The Washington Post. Retrieved February 26, 2017 from http://www.washingtonpost.com/repeal-of-glass-steagall-not-a-cause-but-a-multiplier/2012/08/02/gJQAuvvRXX_story.html.

[137]Stanley, M. (2016, August 26). There Are Real Reasons to Bring Back Glass-Steagall | American Banker. Retrieved February 26, 2017 from http://www.americanbanker.com/bankthink/there-are-real-reasons-to-bring-back-glass-steagall-1090975-1.html

[138]Stanley, M. (2016, August 26). There Are Real Reasons to Bring

Back Glass-Steagall | American Banker. Retrieved February 26, 2017 from http://www.americanbanker.com/bankthink/there-are-real-reasons-to-bring-back-glass-steagall-1090975-1.html

[139]Stanley, M. (2016, August 26). There Are Real Reasons to Bring Back Glass-Steagall | American Banker. Retrieved February 26, 2017 from http://www.americanbanker.com/bankthink/there-are-real-reasons-to-bring-back-glass-steagall-1090975-1.html.

[140]Martens, P., & Martens, R. (2014, August 7). Dodd-Frank Versus Glass-Steagall. How Do They Compare? Retrieved February 26, 2017 from http://wallstreetonparade.com/2014/08/dodd-frank-versus-glass-steagall-how-do-they-compare/.

[141]Martens, P., & Martens, R. (2014, August 7). Dodd-Frank Versus Glass-Steagall: How Do They Compare? Retrieved February 26, 2017 from http://wallstreetonparade.com/2014/08/dodd-frank-versus-glass-steagall-how-do-they-compare/.

[142]Martens, P., & Martens, R. (2014, August 7). Dodd-Frank Versus Glass-Steagall: How Do They Compare? Retrieved February 26, 2017 from http://wallstreetonparade.com/2014/08/dodd-frank-versus-glass-steagall-how-do-they-compare/.

[143]Martens, P., & Martens, R. (2014, August 7). Dodd-Frank Versus Glass-Steagall: How Do They Compare? Retrieved February 26, 2017 from http://wallstreetonparade.com/2014/08/dodd-frank-versus-glass-steagall-how-do-they-compare/.

[144]Martens, P., & Martens, R. (2014, August 7). Dodd-Frank Versus Glass-Steagall: How Do They Compare? Retrieved February 26, 2017 from http://wallstreetonparade.com/2014/08/dodd-frank-versus-glass-steagall-how-do-they-compare/.

[145]Executive Orders | National Archives. (n.d.). Retrieved Oct. 13. 2016 from https://www.archives.gov/federal-register/codification/executive-order/12631.html
(Note: this website states, "**Source:** The provisions of Executive Order 12631 of Mar. 18, 1988, appear at 53 FR 9421, 3 CFR, 1988 Comp., p. 559, unless otherwise noted."

[146] Whitney, M. (2007, March 7). Juicing the Stock Market; the secret maneuverings of the Plunge Protection Team. Retrieved February 26, 2017 from http://www.informationclearinghouse.info/article17251.htm.

[147]Crudele, J. (2010, February 11). Plot thickens in the battle of 'The Plunge' | New York Post. Retrieved March 1, 2017 from

http://nypost.com/2010/02/11/plot-thickens-in-the-battle-of-the-plunge/.

[148]Crudele, J. (2010, February 11). Plot thickens in the battle of 'The Plunge' | New York Post. Retrieved March 1, 2017 from http://nypost.com/2010/02/11/plot-thickens-in-the-battle-of-the-plunge/.

[149]Crudele, J. (2010, February 11). Plot thickens in the battle of 'The Plunge' | New York Post. Retrieved March 1, 2017 from http://nypost.com/2010/02/11/plot-thickens-in-the-battle-of-the-plunge/.

[150]Durden, T. (2015, February 23). *Ex-Plunge Protection Team Whistleblower: "Governments Control Markets; There Is No Price Discovery Anymore"* | Zero Hedge. Retrieved March 1, 2017 from http://www.zerohedge.com/news/2015-02-23/ex-plunge-protection-team-whistleblower-governments-control-markets-there-no-price-d (Note: Website includes apparent video/picture)/audio. This website states, "In this 38 minute interview Lars Schall, for Matterhorn Asset Management, speaks with Dr Pippa Malmgren, a US financial advisor and policy expert based in London. Dr Malmgren has been a member of the U.S. President's Working Group on Financial Markets (a.k.a. the "Plunge Protection Team"). They address, inter alia: Malmgren's recent book 'Signals: the breakdown of the social contract and the rise of geopolitics' ....")
(Note: Tyler Durden might be a pen name or pseudonym. The Business Insider website states in part, "[Tyler Durden is] the pseudonym for Zero Hedge's key author(s) used to hide their identities." Tyler Durden - Business Insider. (n.d.). Retrieved March 1, 2017 from http://www.businessinsider.com/author/tyler-durden)

[151]Durden, T. (2015, February 23). *Ex-Plunge Protection Team Whistleblower: "Governments Control Markets; There Is No Price Discovery Anymore"* | Zero Hedge. Retrieved March 1, 2017 from http://www.zerohedge.com/news/2015-02-23/ex-plunge-protection-team-whistleblower-governments-control-markets-there-no-price-d (Note: Website includes apparent video/picture)/audio. This website states, "In this 38 minute interview Lars Schall, for Matterhorn Asset Management, speaks with Dr Pippa Malmgren, a US financial advisor and policy expert based in London. Dr Malmgren has been a member of the U.S. President's Working Group on Financial Markets (a.k.a. the "Plunge Protection Team"). They address, inter alia: Malmgren's recent book 'Signals: the breakdown of the social contract and the rise of geopolitics' ....")

(Note: Tyler Durden might be a pen name or pseudonym. The Business Insider website states in part, "[Tyler Durden is] the pseudonym for Zero Hedge's key author(s) used to hide their identities." Tyler Durden - Business Insider. (n.d.). Retrieved March 1, 2017 from http://www.businessinsider.com/author/tyler-durden)

[152]Brown, E. H. (2007, 2008). *Web of debt: The shocking truth about our money system and how we can break free* Baton Rouge, LA, Third Millennium Press (pp. 5-6).

[153]Definition of Petrodollars. (n.d.). Retrieved February 26, 2017 from http://faculty.georgetown.edu/imo3/petrod/define.htm.

[154]Robinson, J. (n.d.). Preparing for the Collapse of the Petrodollar System. Retrieved February 26, 2017 from https://ftmdaily.com/preparing-for-the-collapse-of-the-petrodollar-system/

[155]About the IMF. (n.d.). Retrieved February 26, 2017 from http://www.imf.org/external/about.htm

[156]About the IMF. (n.d.). Retrieved February 26, 2017 from http://www.imf.org/external/about.htm

[157]About the IMF. (n.d.). Retrieved February 26, 2017 from http://www.imf.org/external/about.htm

[158]About the IMF. (n.d.). Retrieved February 26, 2017 from http://www.imf.org/external/about.htm

[159]History. (n.d.). Retrieved February 26, 2017 from http://www.worldbank.org/en/about/history

[160]History. (n.d.). Retrieved February 26, 2017 from http://www.worldbank.org/en/about/history

[161] History. (n.d.). Retrieved February 26, 2017 from http://www.worldbank.org/en/about/history

[162]Katusa, M. (2014, May 29). *'Colder War' and the end of the petrodollar.* Retrieved February 26, 2017 from https://www.forbes.com/sites/energysource/2014/05/29/the-colder-war-and-the-end-of-the-petrodollar/#47fdc92866de

[163]Izquierdo, S. (2014, July 16). *BRICS Nations To Form Bank To Rival World Bank, IMF* | The Huffington Post. Retrieved January 21, 2015 from http://www.huffingtonpost.com/2014/07/16/brics-nations-bank_n_5591436.html
(Note: While editing this book on February 26, 2017, I noticed that The Huffington Post website no longer has this article.)

[164]Hartley, J. (2014, July 28). *The BRICS Bank is born out of politics.* Retrieved February 26, 2017 from https://www.forbes.com/sites/jonhartley/2014/07/28/the-brics-bank-is-born-out-of-politics/#11ae2c715bfe

[165]Hartley, J. (2014, July 28). *The BRICS Bank is born out of politics.* Retrieved February 26, 2017 from https://www.forbes.com/sites/jonhartley/2014/07/28/the-brics-bank-is-born-out-of-politics/#11ae2c715bfe

[166]Special Drawing Right SDR. (n.d.). Retrieved Oct. 22, 2016 from https://www.imf.org/en/About/Factsheets/Sheets/2016/08/01/14/51/Special-Drawing-Right-SDR

[167]Chinese Yuan's Ascent to Global Reserve Status: A Timeline - Bloomberg. (n.d.). Retrieved February 26, 2017 from https://www.bloomberg.com/news/articles/2016-09-29/the-chinese-yuan-s-march-to-global-reserve-status-a-timeline. (Note: At the bottom of this online Bloomberg article, it states, "*With assistance by Robin Ganguly, Wenwen Zhang, and Helen Sun.*")

[168]Paul, R. (2009). *End the Fed.* New York, NY: Grand Central Publishing (a division of Hachette Book Group, Inc.) (p. 198). (Copyright by The Foundation for Rational Economics and Education, Inc.)

[169]Brown, E. H. (2007, 2008). *Web of debt: The shocking truth about our money system and how we can break free* Baton Rouge, LA, Third Millennium Press (p.1-2).

[170]Franklin, B. (2016). *Benjamin Franklin's Book of virtues.* Carlisle, MA: Applewood Books.

[171]Franklin, B. (2016). *Benjamin Franklin's Book of virtues.* Carlisle, MA: Applewood Books. (p.14) (Note: Capitalization as in text of book.)

[172]Washington, G. (1796, September 19). Our Documents - Transcript of President George Washington's Farewell Address (1796). Retrieved February 26, 2017 from https://www.ourdocuments.gov/doc.php?flash=true&doc=15&page=transcript. (Note: Website indicates that the transcription is a courtesy of the Avalon Project at Yale Law School.)

[173]The Constitution of the United States: A Transcription | National Archives. (n.d.). Retrieved from https://www.archives.gov/founding-docs/constitution-transcript

[174]State Applications by Amendment Subject. (n.d.). Retrieved Dec. 18, 2016 from http://www.foavc.org/StateApplications/Amendment_Subject.htm (Note: After this citation was put in this book, the website was updated. The website states, that it was, "LAST UPDATED ON 26-FEBRUARY-2017."

[175]State Applications by Amendment Subject. (n.d.). Retrieved Dec. 18, 2016 from http://www.foavc.org/StateApplications/Amendment_Subject.htm (Note: After this citation was put in this book, the website was updated. The website states, that it was, "LAST UPDATED ON 26-FEBRUARY-2017."

[176]Billups, A. (2014, April 11). 34 States Call for Constitutional Convention — and Possible Rewrite. Retrieved December 18, 2016 from http://www.newsmax.com/US/constitutional-convention-Boehner-balanced-budget/2014/04/11/id/565155/

[177]Van Sickle, T. M., & Boughey, L. M. (1990). Lawful and Peaceful Revolution: Article V and Congress' Present Duty to Call a Convention for Proposing Amendments. Hamline Law Review, 14(1), 1-115. Retrieved December 18, 2016, from http://www.foa5c.org/01page/Articles/Articles.htm#LynnBoughey (Note: Online article in 3 PDFs. See p.40)

[178]10 Insanely Overpaid Public Employees | The Fiscal Times. (n.d.). Retrieved February 26, 2017 from http://www.thefiscaltimes.com/Media/Slideshow/2011/07/13/10-Insanely-Overpaid-Public-Employees?page=9

[179]Contribution and Benefit Base. (n.d.). Retrieved February 27, 2017 from https://www.ssa.gov/OACT/COLA/cbb.html#Series

[180]Scientists breed goats that produce spider silk. (2010, May 31). Retrieved December 16, 2016 from https://phys.org/news/2010-05-scientists-goats-spider-silk.html

[181]Declaration of Independence: A Transcription | National Archives. (1776, July 4). Retrieved February 27, 2017 from https://www.archives.gov/founding-docs/declaration-transcript

[182]Federal Citizen Information Center: Our Flag. (n.d.). Retrieved February 07, 2017, from https://publications.usa.gov/epublications/ourflag/pledge.htm

[183]Proverbs 3:5-6 KJV - Bible Gateway. (n.d.). Retrieved February 26, 2017 from https://www.biblegateway.com/passage/?search=Proverbs+3%3A5-6&version=KJV

(Note: Website includes the words "King James Version (KJV) Public Domain.")

[184] Matthew 22:35-40 KJV - Bible Gateway. (n.d.). Retrieved February 26, 2017 from https://www.biblegateway.com/passage/?search=++Matthew+22%3A35-40&version=KJV (Note: Website includes the words "King James Version (KJV) Public Domain.")

[185] Declaration of Independence: A Transcription | National Archives. (n.d.). Retrieved on February 26, 2017 https://www.archives.gov/founding-docs/declaration-transcript

[186] The Constitution of the United States: A Transcription | National Archives. (n.d.). Retrieved from https://www.archives.gov/founding-docs/constitution-transcript

[187] The New United States of America Adopted the Bill of Rights. (n.d.). Retrieved February 27, 2017 from http://www.americaslibrary.gov/jb/nation/jb_nation_bofright_1.html

[188] The New United States of America Adopted the Bill of Rights. (n.d.). Retrieved February 27, 2017 from http://www.americaslibrary.gov/jb/nation/jb_nation_bofright_1.html

[189] The Bill of Rights: A Transcription | National Archives. (n.d.). Retrieved February 27, 2017 from https://www.archives.gov/founding-docs/bill-of-rights-transcript

[190] The Bill of Rights: A Transcription | National Archives. (n.d.). Retrieved February 27, 2017 from https://www.archives.gov/founding-docs/bill-of-rights-transcript

[191] The Constitution: Amendments 11-27. (n.d.). Retrieved February 27, 2017 from https://www.archives.gov/founding-docs/amendments-11-27

[192] Washington, G. (1796, September 19). Our Documents - Transcript of President George Washington's Farewell Address (1796). Retrieved February 26, 2017 from https://www.ourdocuments.gov/doc.php?flash=true&doc=15&page=transcript. (Note: Website indicates that the transcription is a courtesy of the Avalon Project at Yale Law School.)

[193] Lincoln, A. (n.d.). Transcript of Gettysburg Address (1863) (print-friendly version). Retrieved February 26, 2017 from https://www.ourdocuments.gov/print_friendly.php?flash=true&page=transcript&doc=36&title=Transcript+of+Gettysburg+Address+ (1863) (Note: Website states, "Abraham Lincoln, Draft

62477920R00154

Made in the USA
Lexington, KY
08 April 2017